DANIEL'S 70 WEEKS PROPHECY

Dr. Maxwell Shimba

SHIMBA
PUBLISHING

Shimba Publishing LLC
Printed in the United States of America

First Printing Edition, 2024

TABLE OF CONTENTS

INTRODUCTION

Overview of the Book of Daniel

The Book of Daniel is a unique and captivating part of the Old Testament, blending historical narrative with apocalyptic visions. It is named after its main character, Daniel, a young Jewish nobleman taken into Babylonian captivity. Daniel's life spans the reigns of several rulers, from Nebuchadnezzar of Babylon to Cyrus of Persia, highlighting his unwavering faith and God's providence.

The book is divided into two distinct parts:

1. Chapters 1-6: These chapters contain historical narratives, including well-known stories such as Daniel in the lion's den and the fiery furnace.

2. Chapters 7-12: These chapters are apocalyptic visions, filled with symbolic imagery and prophecies concerning future events.

Daniel's prophecies have been a source of hope and intrigue for believers throughout history, offering insights into God's sovereignty and the ultimate triumph of His kingdom.

Historical Context

The Book of Daniel is set during a tumultuous period in Jewish history, beginning with the Babylonian exile in 605 B.C. when King Nebuchadnezzar II of Babylon conquered Jerusalem and deported many Jews, including Daniel and his friends. This period of exile was a significant moment of crisis and transformation for the Jewish people, challenging their faith and identity.

Daniel's life in Babylon was marked by his steadfast commitment to God amidst a pagan culture. He served in high-ranking positions under multiple kings, including Nebuchadnezzar, Belshazzar, Darius the Mede, and Cyrus the Great. Daniel's ability to interpret dreams and visions earned him favor and respect, demonstrating God's power over the kingdoms of men.

Understanding the historical context of Daniel is crucial for interpreting his prophecies. The book reflects the political and spiritual challenges faced by the Jewish people and their longing for divine intervention and restoration.

Importance of Prophecy in the Bible

Prophecy holds a significant place in the Bible, serving as a means through which God communicates His will and plans to humanity. Biblical prophecies often contain messages of warning, judgment, and hope, calling God's people to repentance and faithfulness while assuring them of His ultimate sovereignty and plan for redemption.

Key purposes of biblical prophecy include:

1. Revelation of God's Character: Prophecies reveal God's holiness, justice, mercy, and faithfulness.

2. Guidance and Encouragement: Prophecies provide guidance for living in accordance with God's will and encourage believers to remain steadfast in their faith.

3. Verification of God's Word: The fulfillment of prophecy serves as evidence of the reliability and truthfulness of God's word.

4. Hope for the Future: Prophecies offer hope for the future, pointing to the coming of the Messiah and the establishment of God's eternal kingdom.

Daniel's prophecies, particularly the vision of the seventy weeks, are crucial for understanding God's redemptive plan through history, culminating in the coming of Jesus Christ and the ultimate restoration of all things.

Introduction to Daniel Chapter 9

Daniel Chapter 9 is one of the most significant prophetic chapters in the Bible, containing the prophecy of the seventy weeks. This chapter is set during the first year of Darius the Mede's reign, around 539 B.C. Daniel, having studied the writings of the prophet Jeremiah, realizes that the seventy years of Jerusalem's desolation are nearing completion. This realization leads him to a fervent prayer of confession and supplication on behalf of his people.

Daniel's prayer (verses 1-19) is a heartfelt plea for God's mercy and forgiveness, acknowledging the sins of Israel and seeking God's favor for the restoration of Jerusalem. In response to his prayer, the angel Gabriel appears and delivers the prophecy of the seventy weeks (verses 20-27), outlining God's plan for Israel and the coming of the Messiah.

This prophecy is complex and filled with symbolism, but it provides a detailed timeline of significant events leading to the arrival of the Anointed One and the ultimate fulfillment of God's redemptive purposes. The Seventy Weeks prophecy is pivotal for understanding the overarching narrative of salvation history and God's dealings with His people.

DR. MAXWELL SHIMBA

CHAPTER
01

THE CONTEXT OF DANIEL'S PROPHECY

The Exile and Daniel's Role in Babylon

The Babylonian exile, which began in 605 B.C., was a profound and transformative period for the Jewish people. This exile was a direct consequence of their disobedience to God, as repeatedly warned by the prophets. The fall of Jerusalem and the deportation of its inhabitants to Babylon marked the beginning of seventy years of captivity.

Daniel, a young nobleman, was among the first wave of exiles taken to Babylon. Despite being in a foreign land, Daniel distinguished himself by his unwavering faith and commitment to God's laws. Along with his friends Hananiah, Mishael, and Azariah (better known by their Babylonian names Shadrach, Meshach, and Abednego), Daniel resolved not to defile himself with the royal food and wine, earning favor and wisdom from God (Daniel 1:8-20).

Daniel's extraordinary ability to interpret dreams and visions brought him to the attention of King Nebuchadnezzar, who appointed him to high positions within the Babylonian administration. This favor continued under subsequent rulers, including Belshazzar, Darius the Mede, and Cyrus the Persian. Daniel's integrity and prophetic insight made him a pivotal figure in the courts of these powerful kings, demonstrating God's sovereignty over the nations.

Daniel's Prayer and Confession (Daniel 9:1-19)

In the first year of Darius the Mede's reign, Daniel turned to the writings of the prophet Jeremiah and realized that the seventy years of Jerusalem's desolation were drawing to a close (Daniel 9:2). Moved by this revelation, Daniel engaged in a heartfelt prayer of confession and supplication, seeking God's mercy for his people.

Daniel 9:1-19 records this profound prayer, which is notable for its humility, sincerity, and theological depth. Daniel begins by acknowledging God's greatness and faithfulness, contrasting it with Israel's sin and rebellion. He confesses the collective sins of the people, and their leaders, and even includes himself in this confession, demonstrating solidarity and repentance.

Key elements of Daniel's prayer include:

1. Confession of Sin: Daniel openly acknowledges the sins of Israel, their failure to obey God's commandments and the resulting consequences.

2. Appeal to God's Mercy: Daniel pleads for God's mercy, not based on the righteousness of the people but on God's great compassion and covenantal promises.

3. Petition for Restoration: Daniel asks God to turn His wrath away from Jerusalem, His holy city, and to restore the desolate sanctuary.

This prayer highlights the essential components of true repentance: recognition of sin, confession, and an appeal for divine mercy. Daniel's prayer serves as a model for believers, illustrating the power of intercessory prayer and the importance of aligning one's requests with God's will and promises.

The Arrival of Gabriel

While Daniel was still in prayer, the angel Gabriel was sent to give him insight and understanding concerning the future of his people and the holy city. Gabriel's sudden arrival underscores the urgency and significance of the message he is about to deliver.

Gabriel first reassures Daniel of his esteemed status before God, acknowledging his earnestness in seeking divine understanding (Daniel 9:23). This affirmation serves to highlight Daniel's faithfulness and the sincerity of his prayer.

The prophecy Gabriel delivers, known as the prophecy of the seventy weeks (Daniel 9:24-27), is a detailed revelation of God's redemptive timeline. Gabriel explains that seventy-sevens' are decreed for Daniel's people and the holy city to accomplish six key objectives, which include finishing transgression, putting an end to sin, atoning for wickedness, bringing in everlasting righteousness, sealing up vision and prophecy, and anointing the Most Holy Place.

This prophetic message is dense with symbolism and requires careful interpretation. It outlines the period from the decree to restore and rebuild Jerusalem to the coming of the Anointed One and the ultimate fulfillment of God's plan for Israel.

Gabriel's message to Daniel is both a response to his prayer and a profound revelation of God's sovereign plan. It reassures Daniel that despite the present desolation, God's purposes will prevail, and a glorious future awaits.

CHAPTER

02

UNDERSTANDING BIBLICAL PROPHECY

Prophetic Literature in the Bible

Prophetic literature is a significant and distinctive genre within the Bible, encompassing books that convey God's messages through His chosen prophets. These messages often include warnings, calls to repentance, promises of restoration, and revelations about future events. Prophetic books are found in both the Old and New Testaments, and they play a crucial role in the biblical narrative.

Key characteristics of biblical prophecy include:

1. Divine Origin: Prophets are chosen and inspired by God to deliver His messages. Their words are seen as authoritative and binding because they come directly from God.

2. Foretelling and Forthtelling: Prophets not only predict future events (foretelling) but also speak to the current spiritual, moral, and social conditions of their time (forthtelling).

3. Symbolism and Imagery: Prophetic messages often use vivid imagery and symbolic language to convey deeper spiritual truths and future realities.

4. Conditional and Unconditional Prophecies: Some prophecies are conditional, depending on the response of the people (e.g., Jonah's prophecy to Nineveh), while others are unconditional, revealing God's sovereign plan regardless of human actions (e.g., the promise of the Messiah).

The prophetic books can be divided into major prophets (Isaiah, Jeremiah, Ezekiel, and Daniel) and minor prophets (Hosea through Malachi). Each prophet addresses specific historical contexts and challenges, yet their messages often transcend their immediate circumstances, pointing to broader theological themes and future fulfillments.

Symbolism and Numbers in Prophecy

Symbolism and numbers are integral to understanding biblical prophecy. They provide a rich tapestry of meaning that transcends literal interpretation, inviting readers to explore deeper spiritual truths.

Common symbols in biblical prophecy include:

- Animals: Represent nations, leaders, or spiritual forces (e.g., the lion and the lamb, the beasts in Daniel and Revelation).

- Numbers: Convey completeness, perfection, or specific periods of time (e.g., 7 signifies completeness, 40 denotes a period of testing or judgment).

- Colors: Symbolize various attributes or conditions (e.g., white for purity, red for bloodshed or war, black for mourning or famine).

- Objects: Represent spiritual realities or divine actions (e.g., the sword symbolizes judgment, the lampstand signifies the presence of God).

Understanding the symbolic nature of these elements is essential for interpreting prophetic texts accurately. The use of numbers, in particular, requires careful consideration of their symbolic meanings rather than just their numerical value.

The Concept of Weeks in Biblical Context

In biblical prophecy, the term "weeks" often signifies a set period of seven years rather than seven days. This use of "weeks" as units of time, known as "heptads," is crucial for interpreting the seventy-week prophecy in Daniel.

The concept of weeks can be understood in several contexts:

1. Creation Week: The seven-day creation account in Genesis sets the precedent for a week as a complete unit of time.

2. Sabbatical Cycle: In Leviticus 25, the land is to rest every seventh year, establishing a cycle of seven-year periods.

3. Year of Jubilee: Every fiftieth year, following seven cycles of seven years, is a Jubilee year, marking a time of release and restoration (Leviticus 25:8-13).

In Daniel 9:24-27, the "seventy weeks" are understood as seventy sets of seven years, totaling 490 years. This period is divided into three segments: seven weeks (49 years), sixty-two weeks (434 years), and one week (7 years). Each segment represents significant phases in God's redemptive plan for Israel and the world.

The interpretation of these weeks involves recognizing the symbolic and historical significance of the numbers, as well as their fulfillment in the context of biblical prophecy. Understanding the use of weeks in this way allows for a more profound appreciation of the prophetic timeline and God's overarching plan.

03

THE SEVENTY WEEKS EXPLAINED (DANIEL 9:24)

Analysis of Daniel 9:24

Daniel 9:24 (NIV): "Seventy 'sevens' are decreed for your people and your holy city to finish transgression, to put an end to sin, to atone for wickedness, to bring in everlasting righteousness, to seal up vision and prophecy and to anoint the Most Holy Place."

This verse is the cornerstone of the seventy-week prophecy. Gabriel reveals to Daniel that seventy 'sevens'—or seventy weeks of years (490 years)—have been decreed for the Jewish people and Jerusalem. This period is designed to accomplish specific divine purposes.

The Purpose of the Seventy Weeks

The seventy-week prophecy outlines God's timeline for fulfilling His redemptive plan for Israel and, by extension, the world. This period is intended to address the consequences of sin, bring about restoration, and fulfill God's promises. It is divided into three distinct periods: seven weeks (49 years), sixty-two weeks (434 years), and one final week (7 years). Together, these periods total 490 years, each segment marking significant events in redemptive history.

The purpose of the seventy weeks can be understood through the six specific objectives listed in Daniel 9:24. Each of these objectives is a critical component of God's overarching plan.

Six Objectives of the Seventy Weeks

1. To Finish Transgression

- This objective involves bringing an end to Israel's rebellion and disobedience. Throughout their history, the Israelites repeatedly turned away from God, leading to their exile and suffering. The prophecy indicates a future time when this cycle of transgression will be brought to a close, signifying a renewed covenantal relationship between God and His people.

2. To Put an End to Sin

- Sin, as a fundamental barrier between humanity and God, will be decisively dealt with. This speaks to the ultimate solution to sin, which is found in the sacrificial death of Jesus Christ. By His atoning sacrifice, the power and penalty of sin are broken, allowing believers to live in righteousness.

3. To Atone for Wickedness

- Atonement is central to the redemption process. This objective was fulfilled through Jesus' crucifixion, where He bore the sins of humanity and provided the means for reconciliation with God. The atonement covers the wickedness of both Israel and all who place their faith in Christ.

4. To Bring in Everlasting Righteousness

- This refers to the establishment of a new order of righteousness that will endure forever. Through the Messiah's work, a state of righteousness is inaugurated, ultimately to be fully realized in His second coming. This everlasting righteousness signifies the restoration of all things to their intended state of holiness and justice.

5. To Seal Up Vision and Prophecy

- This objective implies the completion and fulfillment of all prophetic visions and messages. The prophecy concerning the Messiah and the restoration of Israel, as well as other biblical prophecies, will be fulfilled, confirming the truth and reliability of God's word. "Sealing up" suggests that the purpose of the prophecies has been achieved, leaving no further need for additional prophetic revelation concerning these events.

6. To Anoint the Most Holy Place

- The anointing of the Most Holy Place likely refers to the consecration of a new temple or the establishment of God's holy presence among His people. While this has various interpretations, it can symbolize the ultimate sanctification of God's dwelling place, whether viewed as a physical temple or the eschatological dwelling of God with His people in the New Jerusalem.

Each of these objectives points to a comprehensive plan of redemption that addresses the problem of sin, provides a means of atonement, establishes a new order of righteousness, and fulfills God's prophetic promises. The seventy-week prophecy, therefore, encapsulates the essence of God's plan for human history, focusing particularly on the role of the Messiah and the ultimate restoration of His people.

Daniel 9:24 Commentary:

An expository study and comprehensive commentary on Daniel 9:24 using the King James Bible.

Verse 24:

"Seventy weeks are determined upon thy people and upon thy holy city, to finish the transgression, and to make an end of sins, and to make reconciliation for iniquity, and to bring in everlasting righteousness, and to seal up the vision and prophecy, and to anoint the most Holy."

King James Bible's Reference:

"Seventy weeks are determined upon thy people and upon thy holy city, to finish the transgression, and to make an end of sins, and to make reconciliation for iniquity, and to bring in everlasting righteousness, and to seal up the vision and prophecy, and to anoint the most Holy." (Daniel 9:24, KJV)

Interpretation:

In this verse, the angel Gabriel delivers a prophecy to Daniel concerning the future of Israel and Jerusalem. The "seventy weeks" (often understood as seventy 'sevens' or seventy sets of seven years) are decreed for several significant purposes related to the spiritual restoration and ultimate redemption of God's people.

Commentary:

"Seventy weeks are determined upon thy people and upon thy holy city": The term "weeks" here is generally understood to mean sets of seven years, making seventy weeks equivalent to 490 years. This period is specifically allocated for the people of Israel (Daniel's people) and Jerusalem (Daniel's holy city). This long-term prophecy spans from the time of Daniel to the coming of the Messiah and beyond.

"To finish the transgression": This phrase indicates the culmination of Israel's transgressions or rebellions against God. It suggests a time when their persistent sin will be brought to an end (Isaiah 53:5).

"And to make an end of sins": This points to a future time when sin will be completely eradicated. The phrase can be seen as a prophecy of the ultimate victory over sin through the atoning work of Jesus Christ (Hebrews 9:26).

"And to make reconciliation for iniquity": This refers to the atonement for sin, a central theme in Christian theology fulfilled by Christ's sacrificial death on the cross (Romans 5:10).

"And to bring in everlasting righteousness": The prophecy speaks of a time when eternal righteousness will be established. This is often interpreted as the reign of Christ, where righteousness and justice prevail (2 Peter 3:13).

"And to seal up the vision and prophecy": This signifies the fulfillment and completion of all prophecies concerning Israel and the Messiah. Once these events occur, the prophecies will be fully realized and authenticated (Revelation 10:7).

"And to anoint the most Holy": This likely refers to the anointing of the Most Holy Place in the new temple or symbolically to the anointing of Jesus as the Messiah (Hebrews 9:24).

Concordance:

- Seventy weeks are determined: This period of seventy sets of seven years, or 490 years, is a prophetic timeline significant to Israel's history and future (Daniel 9:25).

- To finish the transgression: The end of Israel's transgressions points to a future reconciliation with God (Isaiah 53:5).

- To make an end of sins: This indicates the ultimate victory over sin, achieved through Christ (Hebrews 9:26).

- To make reconciliation for iniquity: The atonement for sin is fulfilled in Jesus Christ (Romans 5:10).

- To bring in everlasting righteousness: The establishment of eternal righteousness is associated with the reign of Christ (2 Peter 3:13).

- To seal up the vision and prophecy: The fulfillment of all prophetic visions and messages (Revelation 10:7).

- To anoint the most Holy: The anointing of the Most Holy Place or the Messiah (Hebrews 9:24).

References from the King James Bible:

1. Daniel 9:25: "Know therefore and understand, that from the going forth of the commandment to restore and to build Jerusalem unto the Messiah the Prince shall be seven weeks, and threescore and two weeks: the street shall be built again, and the wall, even in troublous times."

2. Isaiah 53:5: "But he was wounded for our transgressions, he was bruised for our iniquities: the chastisement of our peace was upon him; and with his stripes we are healed."

3. Hebrews 9:26: "For then must he often have suffered since the foundation of the world: but now once in the end of the world hath he appeared to put away sin by the sacrifice of himself."

4. Romans 5:10: "For if, when we were enemies, we were reconciled to God by the death of his Son, much more, being reconciled, we shall be saved by his life."

5. 2 Peter 3:13: "Nevertheless we, according to his promise, look for new heavens and a new earth, wherein dwelleth righteousness."

6. Revelation 10:7: "But in the days of the voice of the seventh angel, when he shall begin to sound, the mystery of God should be finished, as he hath declared to his servants the prophets."

7. Hebrews 9:24: "For Christ is not entered into the holy places made with hands, which are the figures of the true;

but into heaven itself, now to appear in the presence of God for us:"

Interpretation and Application:

- Prophetic Timeline: Understanding the "seventy weeks" as a prophetic timeline encourages believers to study and reflect on the fulfillment of God's promises through history and into the future.

- Atonement and Reconciliation: This verse highlights the centrality of Christ's atonement and the promise of reconciliation with God, underscoring key aspects of Christian faith.

- Eternal Righteousness: The promise of everlasting righteousness gives hope for a future where God's justice and righteousness will prevail, inspiring believers to live in anticipation of Christ's return.

The implications of Daniel 9:24 for the early Church are profound and multifaceted, impacting theological understanding, ecclesiastical identity, and eschatological expectations.

Theological Implications

1. Christocentric Fulfillment:

The early Church would have seen the prophecy in Daniel 9:24 as a direct reference to the mission and work of Jesus Christ. The phrase "to make an end of sins" and "to make reconciliation for iniquity" clearly align with the atoning sacrifice of Jesus on the cross, which was a cornerstone of early Christian doctrine. This fulfillment reinforces the belief in Jesus as the Messiah prophesied in the Old Testament.

2. Establishment of Everlasting Righteousness:

The prophecy's promise to "bring in everlasting righteousness" would resonate with early Christians as a realization of the new covenant. This covenant, characterized by the indwelling Holy Spirit and the transformative power of grace, marked a departure from the old covenant's reliance on the Law. It also affirmed the theological transition from the age of the Law to the age of grace through faith in Christ.

Ecclesiastical Implications

1. Validation of Apostolic Teaching:

The early Church relied heavily on the fulfillment of Old Testament prophecies to validate the teachings of the apostles. Daniel 9:24 served as a critical text in demonstrating that Jesus' life, death, and resurrection were in accordance with God's predetermined plan. This bolstered the apostolic authority and provided a scriptural foundation for their preaching.

2. Unified Identity:

The early Church, composed of both Jewish and Gentile believers, found in this prophecy a unifying identity. For Jewish converts, it confirmed that their historical faith and scriptures pointed to Jesus as the fulfillment of God's promises. For Gentile converts, it provided a theological grounding that integrated them into the salvific history of Israel, fostering a sense of inclusion and shared destiny.

Eschatological Implications

1. Expectation of Christ's Return:

Daniel 9:24's reference to the sealing up of "the vision and prophecy" and the anointing of "the most Holy" would be interpreted as partially fulfilled in Christ's first coming, with complete fulfillment anticipated in His second coming.

The early Church lived in constant expectation of Christ's imminent return, which influenced their eschatological teachings and urgency in evangelism.

2. Hope in Persecution:

In times of persecution, the early Church drew hope from prophecies like Daniel 9:24. The promise of a future characterized by everlasting righteousness provided a powerful assurance that despite current sufferings, God's ultimate plan would prevail. This eschatological hope was vital in sustaining the faith of early Christians facing trials and martyrdom.

Missiological Implications

1. Prophetic Fulfillment as Evangelistic Tool:

The early Church used the fulfillment of prophecies, such as Daniel 9:24, as a compelling argument in their evangelistic efforts. By demonstrating how Jesus fulfilled these ancient prophecies, they could effectively argue the legitimacy and truth of the Christian faith to both Jews and Gentiles.

2. Motivation for Holiness and Mission:

The understanding that the prophecy includes the establishment of "everlasting righteousness" motivated the early Church towards personal holiness and mission. Believers were encouraged to live righteous lives as a testimony to the transformative power of the gospel and to actively participate in the Church's mission to spread the message of reconciliation and redemption.

Conclusion

Daniel 9:24 provided a rich tapestry of implications for the early Church, influencing their theology, communal identity, eschatological hope, and missiological strategies. It affirmed the fulfillment of God's redemptive plan in Jesus Christ, validated apostolic teaching, and inspired the early Christians to live with a sense of purpose and urgency in anticipation of Christ's return. This prophecy, therefore, played a pivotal role in shaping the faith and practice of the nascent Christian community.

CHAPTER

04

THE FIRST SEVEN WEEKS (DANIEL 9:25)

Historical Fulfillment of the First Seven Weeks

Daniel 9:25 (NIV): "Know and understand this: From the time the word goes out to restore and rebuild Jerusalem until the Anointed One, the ruler, comes, there will be seven 'sevens,' and sixty-two 'sevens.' It will be rebuilt with streets and a trench but in times of trouble."

The first segment of the seventy-week prophecy is the seven 'sevens,' or forty-nine years. This period begins with the decree to restore and rebuild Jerusalem. Historical records and biblical texts provide evidence of this decree and the subsequent rebuilding efforts.

The Command to Restore and Rebuild Jerusalem

The command to restore and rebuild Jerusalem marks the starting point of the seventy-week prophecy. There were several key decrees made by Persian kings that facilitated the return of the Jewish exiles and the reconstruction of Jerusalem:

1. Cyrus' Decree (538 B.C.): King Cyrus of Persia issued a decree allowing the Jews to return to Jerusalem and rebuild the temple (Ezra 1:1-4). This decree was significant as it initiated the process of restoration.

2. Darius' Decree (520 B.C.): King Darius reaffirmed Cyrus' decree, supporting the continuation of the temple reconstruction after opposition had halted the work (Ezra 6:1-12).

3. Artaxerxes' Decree to Ezra (458 B.C.): King Artaxerxes I granted Ezra the authority to return to Jerusalem with a group of exiles and provided resources for the temple services and governance (Ezra 7:11-26).

4. Artaxerxes' Decree to Nehemiah (445 B.C.): This decree specifically authorized Nehemiah to rebuild the walls of Jerusalem (Nehemiah 2:1-8). Nehemiah's efforts were crucial for the physical and spiritual restoration of the city.

The decree to Nehemiah in 445 B.C. is often considered the most fitting starting point for the seventy-week prophecy, given its specific focus on rebuilding Jerusalem's infrastructure.

The Role of Nehemiah and Ezra

The books of Nehemiah and Ezra in the Old Testament provide detailed accounts of the challenges and successes encountered during the restoration of Jerusalem.

1. Nehemiah's Role:

- Rebuilding the Walls: Nehemiah, serving as the cupbearer to King Artaxerxes, received permission to return to Jerusalem and oversee the reconstruction of its walls. Despite significant opposition from surrounding enemies, Nehemiah led the people with determination and faith, completing the walls in fifty-two days (Nehemiah 6:15-16).

- Spiritual Reforms: Nehemiah also implemented spiritual and social reforms to restore the community's commitment to the Mosaic law. He addressed issues such as Sabbath observance, intermarriage, and social injustices (Nehemiah 5, 13).

- Leadership and Governance: Nehemiah's leadership was marked by integrity, prayerfulness, and a deep commitment to God's commands. His efforts laid the foundation for a revitalized and secure Jerusalem.

2. Ezra's Role:

- Teaching the Law: Ezra, a scribe and priest, arrived in Jerusalem before Nehemiah and played a critical role in the spiritual renewal of the people. He was dedicated to teaching the Torah and reestablishing religious practices (Ezra 7:10).

- Covenant Renewal: Under Ezra's leadership, the people engaged in a public reading of the law, followed by a solemn assembly and renewal of the covenant with God (Nehemiah 8-10). This event was pivotal in reorienting the community towards faithful observance of God's commands.

- Addressing Intermarriage: Ezra confronted the issue of intermarriage with pagan inhabitants, which was leading the Israelites away from their covenantal obligations. He led the people in a collective confession and commitment to separate from these influences (Ezra 9-10).

Together, Nehemiah and Ezra's leadership during this period exemplified the integration of physical reconstruction and spiritual revival. Their combined efforts ensured that the restoration of Jerusalem was not only about rebuilding walls but also about reestablishing a community centered on God's law and covenant.

Chapter 9:25 Commentary:

An expository study and comprehensive commentary on Daniel 9:25 using the King James Bible.

Verse 25:

"Know therefore and understand, that from the going forth of the commandment to restore and to build Jerusalem unto the Messiah the Prince shall be seven weeks, and threescore and two weeks: the street shall be built again, and the wall, even in troublous times."

King James Bible's Reference:

"Know therefore and understand, that from the going forth of the commandment to restore and to build Jerusalem unto the Messiah the Prince shall be seven weeks, and threescore and two weeks: the street shall be built again, and the wall, even in troublous times." (Daniel 9:25, KJV)

Interpretation:

In this verse, Gabriel provides Daniel with a detailed timeline for significant future events. The prophecy indicates that a specific period will elapse from the issuing of a decree to restore and rebuild Jerusalem until the coming of the Messiah, the Prince. This period is broken down into two segments: seven weeks and sixty-two weeks, totaling sixty-nine weeks. The rebuilding will occur in difficult circumstances.

Commentary:

"Know therefore and understand": Gabriel emphasizes the importance of understanding the prophecy, indicating that it holds significant meaning for Daniel and the people of Israel (Daniel 9:23).

"That from the going forth of the commandment to restore and to build Jerusalem": This phrase refers to a decree issued to rebuild Jerusalem. Various decrees could be in view, but the most commonly accepted is the decree by Artaxerxes in 445 B.C. (Nehemiah 2:1-8).

"Unto the Messiah, the Prince shall be seven weeks, and threescore and two weeks": The term "weeks" here refers to sets of seven years. Seven weeks (49 years) plus sixty-two weeks (434 years) total 483 years. This timeline predicts the period from the decree to the coming of the Messiah, Jesus Christ (Matthew 1:16).

"The street shall be built again, and the wall, even in troublous times": This part of the prophecy indicates that Jerusalem will be rebuilt, including its streets and walls, despite facing significant opposition and difficulties. This aligns with the historical accounts of Nehemiah's efforts to rebuild Jerusalem amidst considerable resistance (Nehemiah 4:1-23).

Concordance:

- Know therefore and understand: This phrase emphasizes the importance of comprehending the prophecy, indicating its significance for the people of Israel (Daniel 9:23).

- From the going forth of the commandment to restore and to build Jerusalem: This refers to the decree to rebuild Jerusalem, with many scholars identifying the decree by Artaxerxes in 445 B.C. (Nehemiah 2:1-8).

- Unto the Messiah the Prince shall be seven weeks, and threescore and two weeks: This indicates a total of 69 weeks (483 years) from the decree to the coming of the Messiah, Jesus Christ (Matthew 1:16).

- The street shall be built again, and the wall, even in troublous times: This signifies the rebuilding of Jerusalem's streets and walls amidst significant opposition and difficulties (Nehemiah 4:1-23).

References from the King James Bible:

1. Daniel 9:23: "At the beginning of thy supplications the commandment came forth, and I am come to shew thee; for thou art greatly beloved: therefore understand the matter, and consider the vision."

2. Nehemiah 2:1-8: "And it came to pass in the month Nisan, in the twentieth year of Artaxerxes the king, that wine was before him: and I took up the wine, and gave it unto the king. Now I had not been beforetime sad in his presence. Wherefore the king said unto me, Why is thy countenance sad, seeing thou art not sick? this is nothing else but sorrow of heart. Then I was very sore afraid, And said unto the king, Let the king live forever: why should not my countenance be sad, when the city, the place of my fathers' sepulchers, lieth waste, and the gates thereof are consumed with fire? Then the king said unto me, For what dost thou make request? So, I prayed to the God of heaven. And I said unto the king, If it pleases the king, and if thy servant has found favor in thy sight, that thou wouldest send me unto Judah, unto the city of my fathers' sepulchres, that I may build it. And the king said unto me, (the queen also sitting by him,) For how long shall thy journey be? and when wilt thou return? So, it pleased the king to send me; and I set him a time. Moreover, I said unto the king, If it please the king, let letters be given me to the governors beyond the river, that they may convey me over till I come into Judah; And a letter unto Asaph the keeper of the king's forest, that he may give me timber to make beams for the gates of the palace which appertained to the house, and for the wall of the city, and for the house that I shall enter into. And the king granted me, according to the good hand of my God upon me."

3. Matthew 1:16: "And Jacob begat Joseph the husband of Mary, of whom was born Jesus, who is called Christ."

4. Nehemiah 4:1-23: "But it came to pass, that when Sanballat heard that we built the wall, he was wroth, and took great indignation, and mocked the Jews. And he spake before his brethren and the army of Samaria, and said, What do these feeble Jews? will they fortify themselves? will they sacrifice? will they make an end in a day? will they revive the stones out of the heaps of the rubbish which are burned? Now Tobiah the Ammonite was by him, and he said, Even that which they build if a fox go up, he shall even break down their stone wall. Hear, O our God; for we are despised: and turn their reproach upon their own head, and give them for a prey in the land of captivity: And cover not their iniquity, and let not their sin be blotted out from before thee: for they have provoked thee to anger before the builders. So built we the wall; and all the wall was joined together unto the half thereof: for the people had a mind to work. But it came to pass, that when Sanballat, and Tobiah, and the Arabians, and the Ammonites, and the Ashdodites, heard that the walls of Jerusalem were made up, and that the breaches began to be stopped, then they were very wroth, And conspired all of them together to come and to fight against Jerusalem, and to hinder it. Nevertheless we made our prayer unto our God, and set a watch against them day and night, because of them. And Judah said, The strength of the bearers of burdens is decayed, and there is much rubbish; so that we are not able to build the wall. And our adversaries said, They shall not know, neither see, till we come in the midst among them, and slay them, and cause the work to cease. And it came to pass, that when the Jews which dwelt by them came, they said unto us ten times, From all places whence ye shall return unto us they will be upon you.

Therefore, set I in the lower places behind the wall, and on the higher places, I even set the people after their families with their swords, their spears, and their bows. And I looked and rose up, and said unto the nobles, and to the rulers, and to the rest of the people, Be not ye afraid of them: remember the Lord, which is great and terrible, and fight for your brethren, your sons, and your daughters, your wives, and your houses. And it came to pass, when our enemies heard that it was known unto us, and God had brought their counsel to nought, that we returned all of us to the wall, everyone unto his work. And it came to pass from that time forth, that the half of my servants wrought in the work, and the other half of them held both the spears, the shields, and the bows, and the habergeons; and the rulers were behind all the house of Judah. They which builded on the wall, and they that bare burdens, with those that laded, everyone with one of his hands wrought in the work, and with the other hand held a weapon. For the builders, everyone had his sword girded by his side, and so builded. And he that sounded the trumpet was by me. And I said unto the nobles, and to the rulers, and to the rest of the people, The work is great and large, and we are separated upon the wall, one far from another. In what place therefore ye hear the sound of the trumpet, resort ye thither unto us: our God shall fight for us. So we laboured in the work: and half of them held the spears from the rising of the morning till the stars appeared. Likewise at the same time said I unto the people, Let everyone with his servant lodge within Jerusalem, that in the night they may be a guard to us, and labor on the day. So neither I, nor my brethren, nor my servants, nor the men of the guard which followed me, none of us put off our clothes, saving that everyone put them off for washing."

Implications for the Early Church:

1. Validation of Jesus as the Messiah:

- The precise fulfillment of the prophecy regarding the timeline from the decree to rebuild Jerusalem to the coming of the Messiah provided a strong argument for early Christians to validate Jesus as the prophesied Messiah. This prophetic accuracy strengthened the faith of the believers and served as a powerful tool in evangelism.

2. Historical Context for the Christian Faith:

- The prophecy rooted the Christian faith in historical events, linking it directly to the Jewish scriptures and history. This connection helped early Christians understand their faith as a continuation and fulfillment of God's redemptive plan revealed in the Old Testament.

3. Encouragement Amidst Persecution:

- The early Church faced significant opposition and persecution, much like the rebuilding efforts in Jerusalem described in the prophecy. Knowing that God's plan unfolded even amidst troublesome times provided encouragement and a reminder of God's sovereignty and faithfulness.

4. Emphasis on God's Sovereignty:

- The detailed prophecy highlighted God's control over history, reassuring the early Church that God's purposes would be accomplished despite human opposition. This reinforced the belief in God's ultimate authority and providence.

5. Hope and Expectation:

- The prophecy of the Messiah's coming and the establishment of everlasting righteousness fostered a sense of hope and expectation within the early Church. Believers were encouraged to live in anticipation of Christ's return and the fulfillment of God's promises.

The implications of Daniel 9:25 for the early Church:

Implications for the Early Church

1. Validation of Jesus as the Messiah:

The prophecy in Daniel 9:25 provided a precise timeline from the decree to rebuild Jerusalem to the coming of the Messiah. The early Church saw the fulfillment of this prophecy in Jesus Christ, which validated their belief in Him as the prophesied Messiah. This provided a strong foundation for their faith and served as a powerful apologetic tool when engaging with both Jews and Gentiles. The early Christians could point to the fulfillment of this prophecy as evidence that Jesus was indeed the long-awaited Savior.

2. Strengthening of Faith:

The detailed nature of the prophecy and its fulfillment reinforced the faith of early Christians. Knowing that God's promises were being fulfilled according to a divine timeline gave them confidence in the reliability of Scripture and in the faithfulness of God. This was especially important in a time when the Church faced persecution and needed assurance that they were following the true path laid out by God.

3. Historical Continuity:

The prophecy connected the Christian faith to Jewish history and the Scriptures, providing a sense of continuity. Early Christians understood that their faith was not a new religion but the fulfillment of God's redemptive plan revealed throughout the Old Testament. This helped to bridge the gap between Jewish and Gentile believers, fostering unity within the Church.

4. Encouragement Amidst Persecution:

The rebuilding of Jerusalem in "troublous times" mirrored the experiences of the early Church, which faced significant opposition and persecution. The prophecy reminded them that God's plans prevail despite adversity, offering encouragement and strengthening their resolve to remain faithful in the face of trials. It affirmed that God's purposes are accomplished even amidst human opposition and challenges.

5. Emphasis on God's Sovereignty:

The prophecy underscored God's sovereignty over history, reassuring the early Church that God was in control and that their faith was part of His grand design. This assurance helped believers trust God's plan and timing, even when they could not see the immediate outcomes. It reinforced the belief in God's ultimate authority and providence, encouraging them to remain steadfast and obedient.

6. Motivating Holiness and Mission:

The expectation of the Messiah's coming and the establishment of everlasting righteousness motivated the early Christians to live holy lives and to spread the message of the Gospel. They were driven by the hope of Christ's return and the final fulfillment of God's promises, inspiring them to evangelize and disciple others. The sense of urgency and purpose fueled their missionary efforts, as they sought to prepare themselves and others for the coming Kingdom.

7. Eschatological Hope:

The prophecy's reference to the Messiah and the anointing of "the most Holy" pointed to the ultimate fulfillment of God's redemptive plan. This eschatological hope provided a forward-looking perspective, encouraging the early Church to persevere with the expectation that Christ would return and establish His Kingdom in fullness. It gave them a vision of the future that shaped their present actions and attitudes, reinforcing their commitment to living out their faith authentically.

Conclusion

Daniel 9:25 had profound implications for the early Church, shaping their theology, strengthening their faith, and guiding their mission. It validated Jesus as the Messiah, connected their faith to Jewish history, and offered encouragement amidst persecution. It emphasized God's sovereignty, motivated holy living, and fueled their evangelistic efforts. The prophecy provided a framework for understanding their place in God's redemptive plan and instilled a hope that sustained them through trials and tribulations.

CHAPTER

05

THE SIXTY-TWO WEEKS (DANIEL 9:25)

Analysis of the Sixty-Two Weeks

Daniel 9:25 (NIV): "Know and understand this: From the time the word goes out to restore and rebuild Jerusalem until the Anointed One, the ruler, comes, there will be seven 'sevens,' and sixty-two 'sevens.' It will be rebuilt with streets and a trench but in times of trouble."

Following the initial period of seven weeks (49 years) dedicated to the restoration of Jerusalem, the prophecy outlines an additional sixty-two weeks, totaling 434 years. This segment of the prophecy extends from the completion of Jerusalem's rebuilding to the arrival of the Anointed One, the Messiah.

The term "weeks" in this context, as previously established, refers to periods of seven years. Therefore, the sixty-two weeks encompass 434 years, a significant span in the biblical timeline. This period is characterized by anticipation and preparation for the coming of the Anointed One, who plays a pivotal role in God's redemptive plan.

Historical Events and Their Fulfillment

The sixty-two weeks cover a broad and transformative period in Jewish history. Several key events and developments took place during these centuries, laying the groundwork for the Messiah's arrival:

1. Persian Period (539-331 B.C.):

- Rebuilding and Restoration: Following the decrees of Cyrus, Darius, and Artaxerxes, the Jewish exiles returned to their homeland, rebuilt the temple, and reestablished Jerusalem. This period was marked by relative peace and the consolidation of Jewish religious practices.

- Prophets and Writings: Prophets such as Haggai, Zechariah, and Malachi provided guidance and encouragement during the rebuilding process. Their writings also emphasized the coming of a future deliverer and the need for covenantal faithfulness.

2. Hellenistic Period (331-167 B.C.):

- Alexander the Great: The conquest of Alexander the Great brought Hellenistic influence to the region, significantly impacting Jewish culture and society. The spread of the Greek language and thought created a context in which Jewish and Greek ideas interacted.

- The Septuagint: The translation of Hebrew Scriptures into Greek (the Septuagint) occurred during this time, making the Hebrew Scriptures accessible to a broader audience and laying a foundation for the spread of the Gospel.

3. Hasmonean Period (167-63 B.C.):

- Maccabean Revolt: The Jewish revolt against the Seleucid Empire, led by the Maccabees, resulted in a brief period of Jewish independence. The rededication of the temple in 164 B.C. is celebrated in the festival of Hanukkah.

- Hasmonean Dynasty: The Hasmonean rulers established a Jewish state, which, despite internal conflicts, maintained relative independence until the Roman conquest.

4. Roman Period (63 B.C.-70 A.D.):

- Roman Rule: The Roman Empire's control over Judea brought significant political and social changes. The appointment of Herod the Great as king and his extensive building projects, including the expansion of the Second Temple, had lasting impacts.

- Messianic Expectations: This period saw heightened messianic expectations among the Jewish people. Various groups, including the Pharisees, Sadducees, Essenes, and Zealots, reflected diverse responses to Roman rule and hopes for deliverance.

The Coming of the Anointed One

The culmination of the sixty-two weeks is the arrival of the Anointed One, the Messiah. According to Daniel's prophecy, this period leads directly to the manifestation of the promised deliverer, who is identified in the New Testament as Jesus Christ.

1. Historical and Prophetic Fulfillment:

- Jesus of Nazareth: Born around 4 B.C. in Bethlehem, Jesus' life and ministry fulfilled numerous Old Testament prophecies regarding the Messiah. His baptism by John the Baptist, often regarded as His anointing, marked the beginning of His public ministry.

- Public Ministry: Jesus' teachings, miracles, and proclamation of the Kingdom of God aligned with prophetic expectations. His role as the suffering servant, as depicted in Isaiah 53, and His claim to be the Son of God were central to His identity as the Anointed One.

- Crucifixion and Resurrection: Jesus' crucifixion, viewed as the ultimate atoning sacrifice for sin, and His subsequent resurrection are seen as the pivotal events fulfilling the messianic prophecies. These events occurred within the timeline suggested by the sixty-two weeks, affirming the accuracy and divine inspiration of Daniel's prophecy.

2. Theological Implications:

- Redemption and Atonement: The coming of the Anointed One signifies the fulfillment of God's plan for redemption and atonement. Jesus' sacrificial death addressed the problem of sin, providing a way for humanity to be reconciled with God.

- Establishment of the New Covenant: Jesus' ministry inaugurated the New Covenant, characterized by the outpouring of the Holy Spirit and the inclusion of Gentiles into God's redemptive plan. This covenant supersedes the Old Covenant, bringing about a new era of salvation history.

3. Messianic Hope and Fulfillment:

- Hope for Israel and the Nations: The arrival of the Anointed One brought hope not only to Israel but also to the entire world. The message of Jesus Christ transcends ethnic and cultural boundaries, offering salvation to all who believe.

- Future Fulfillment: While Jesus' first coming fulfilled many prophecies, the ultimate consummation of God's plan awaits His second coming. The final fulfillment of all messianic expectations will occur when Jesus returns to establish His eternal kingdom.

CHAPTER

06

THE FINAL WEEK (DANIEL 9:26-27)

The Cutting Off of the Anointed One

Daniel 9:26 (NIV): "After the sixty-two 'sevens,' the Anointed One will be put to death and will have nothing. The people of the ruler who will come will destroy the city and the sanctuary. The end will come like a flood: War will continue until the end, and desolations have been decreed."

The final week of Daniel's prophecy begins with a momentous and tragic event—the cutting off of the Anointed One. This refers to the crucifixion of Jesus Christ, which occurred after the sixty-two weeks, marking the culmination of His earthly ministry.

1. Crucifixion and Its Significance:

- Fulfillment of Prophecy: The death of Jesus on the cross is a direct fulfillment of messianic prophecies. His crucifixion, although seemingly a defeat, was part of God's redemptive plan, bringing about atonement for sin.

- "Having Nothing": This phrase emphasizes the totality of Jesus' sacrifice. He was abandoned, stripped of earthly dignity, and suffered a humiliating death, fulfilling the prophecy of the suffering servant in Isaiah 53.

2. Theological Implications:

- Atonement for Sin: Jesus' death provided the necessary atonement for humanity's sin, reconciling believers to God. This sacrificial act fulfilled the Old Testament sacrificial system and established a new covenant.

- Inauguration of the New Covenant: The crucifixion marked the beginning of the New Covenant, characterized by the indwelling of the Holy Spirit and the extension of God's promises to all nations.

The People of the Prince to Come

Following the cutting off of the Anointed One, the prophecy describes a subsequent period of destruction and turmoil.

1. Destruction of Jerusalem and the Temple:

- Historical Fulfillment: In A.D. 70, the Roman general Titus, leading the forces of the Roman Empire, besieged and destroyed Jerusalem and its temple. This event fulfilled Jesus' own prophecy about the destruction of the temple (Matthew 24:1-2).

- "People of the Ruler Who Will Come": This phrase refers to the Roman forces, often interpreted as representing the broader Roman Empire. The destruction of the city and sanctuary was catastrophic, symbolizing divine judgment.

2. Ongoing Conflict:

- "End Will Come Like a Flood": This imagery conveys the sudden and overwhelming nature of the destruction.

- Continued Desolations: The prophecy indicates that conflict and desolation would persist, reflecting the turbulent history of Jerusalem and the broader region.

The Covenant and the Abomination of Desolation

Daniel 9:27 (NIV): "He will confirm a covenant with many for one 'seven.' In the middle of the 'seven' he will put an end to sacrifice and offering. And at the temple he will set up an abomination that causes desolation, until the end that is decreed is poured out on him."

The final week, or seven-year period, is marked by significant events, including the confirmation of a covenant and the abomination of desolation.

1. Confirmation of the Covenant:

- Interpretations: There are varied interpretations of this covenant. Some view it as a peace treaty or agreement facilitated by a future ruler, while others see it as the establishment of the New Covenant through Christ.

- Implications: The confirmation of the covenant with many suggests a widespread impact, potentially involving both Jews and Gentiles.

2. End of Sacrifice and Offering:

- Midpoint of the Seven: The prophecy indicates that halfway through the final seven-year period, sacrifices and offerings will cease. This cessation could symbolize a significant disruption in religious practices.

- Historical and Future Perspectives: Historically, the destruction of the temple in A.D. 70 ended the Jewish sacrificial system. Futuristically, some interpretations suggest a future event linked to the Antichrist.

3. Abomination of Desolation:

- Historical Event: The phrase "abomination that causes desolation" originally referred to the desecration of the temple by Antiochus IV Epiphanes in 167 B.C. However, Jesus referred to a future fulfillment in Matthew 24:15, indicating an event yet to come.

- Future Fulfillment: Many scholars and theologians believe this prophecy points to an eschatological event involving a future Antichrist figure who will desecrate a rebuilt temple, leading to unprecedented tribulation.

4. End and Judgment:

- Decreed End: The final part of the prophecy declares that the end is decreed and will be poured out on the desolator. This ultimate judgment assures the defeat of evil and the establishment of God's kingdom.

Chapter 9:26 Commentary:

An expository study and comprehensive commentary on Daniel 9:26 using the King James Bible.

Verse 26:

"And after threescore and two weeks shall Messiah be cut off, but not for himself: and the people of the prince that shall come shall destroy the city and the sanctuary; and the end thereof shall be with a flood, and unto the end of the war desolations are determined."

King James Bible's Reference:

"And after threescore and two weeks shall Messiah be cut off, but not for himself: and the people of the prince that shall come shall destroy the city and the sanctuary, and the end thereof shall be with a flood, and unto the end of the war desolations are determined." (Daniel 9:26, KJV)

Interpretation:

In this verse, Gabriel continues to explain the prophetic timeline to Daniel, detailing significant events that will occur after the sixty-two weeks (which follow the initial seven weeks, making a total of sixty-nine weeks or 483 years). The verse addresses the death of the Messiah and the subsequent destruction of Jerusalem and the temple.

Commentary:

"And after threescore and two weeks shall Messiah be cut off, but not for himself": This phrase indicates that after the sixty-two weeks (plus the initial seven weeks), the Messiah will be "cut off," meaning he will be killed. The phrase "but not for himself" suggests that the Messiah's death is not due to his own sins or for his own benefit but for the sake of others, pointing to the atoning sacrifice of Jesus Christ (Isaiah 53:8; John 11:51-52).

"And the people of the prince that shall come shall destroy the city and the sanctuary": This part of the prophecy refers to the destruction of Jerusalem and the temple by the Romans in AD 70. The "people of the prince that shall come" are generally understood to be the Roman forces led by the future Emperor Titus (Matthew 24:2; Luke 19:43-44).

"And the end thereof shall be with a flood": This phrase symbolizes overwhelming destruction and judgment, indicating that the end of Jerusalem will come suddenly and completely (Nahum 1:8).

"And unto the end of the war desolations are determined": The period following the destruction will be marked by continued desolations and war, as determined by God. This indicates a prolonged period of turmoil and suffering (Luke 21:24).

Concordance:

- And after threescore and two weeks shall Messiah be cut off, but not for himself: This phrase predicts the death of the Messiah, indicating his sacrificial death for others (Isaiah 53:8; John 11:51-52).

- And the people of the prince that shall come shall destroy the city and the sanctuary: This prophecy refers to the destruction of Jerusalem and the temple by the Romans in AD 70 (Matthew 24:2; Luke 19:43-44).

- And the end thereof shall be with a flood: This phrase symbolizes sudden and complete destruction, similar to a flood (Nahum 1:8).

- And unto the end of the war desolations are determined: This indicates a prolonged period of desolation and conflict, as decreed by God (Luke 21:24).

References from the King James Bible:

1. Isaiah 53:8: "He was taken from prison and from judgment: and who shall declare his generation? for he was cut off out of the land of the living: for the transgression of my people was he stricken."

2. John 11:51-52: "And this spake he not of himself: but being high priest that year, he prophesied that Jesus should die for that nation; And not for that nation only, but that also he should gather together in one the children of God that were scattered abroad."

3. Matthew 24:2: "And Jesus said unto them, See ye not all these things? verily I say unto you, There shall not be left here one stone upon another, that shall not be thrown down."

4. Luke 19:43-44: "For the days shall come upon thee, that thine enemies shall cast a trench about thee, and compass thee round, and keep thee in on every side, And shall lay thee even with the ground, and thy children within thee; and they shall not leave in thee one stone upon another; because thou knewest not the time of thy visitation."

5. Nahum 1:8: "But with an overrunning flood he will make an utter end of the place thereof, and darkness shall pursue his enemies."

6. Luke 21:24: "And they shall fall by the edge of the sword, and shall be led away captive into all nations: and Jerusalem shall be trodden down of the Gentiles until the times of the Gentiles be fulfilled."

Implications for the Early Church:

1. Understanding of the Messiah's Mission:

- The early Church saw the prophecy of the Messiah being "cut off" as a clear prediction of Jesus' crucifixion. This helped them understand that Jesus' death was part of God's redemptive plan, not a failure but a fulfillment of prophecy, reinforcing the belief in Jesus as the Messiah who came to atone for the sins of humanity.

2. Historical Validation of Prophecy:

- The destruction of Jerusalem and the temple in AD 70 by the Romans was seen as a fulfillment of Daniel's prophecy. This historical event validated the reliability of biblical prophecy and the teachings of Jesus, who also predicted this destruction. It reinforced the early Christians' faith in the divine inspiration of Scripture.

3. Encouragement in Persecution:

- Knowing that the Messiah had to suffer and that Jerusalem would face desolation provided the early Church with a framework for understanding their own sufferings and persecutions. It reassured them that suffering was not outside of God's plan but was part of the larger narrative of redemption and restoration.

4. Eschatological Perspective:

- The reference to continued desolations and wars until the end times gave the early Church an eschatological perspective. They were reminded that current sufferings and turmoil were temporary and that ultimate restoration and peace would come with Christ's return. This perspective helped them endure hardships with hope and perseverance.

5. Call to Holiness and Vigilance:

- The detailed fulfillment of prophecies concerning judgment and desolation served as a sober reminder of God's justice and the seriousness of sin. This called the early Christians to live holy and vigilant lives, remaining faithful to God and obedient to His commandments, knowing that God's judgments are certain and His promises sure.

6. Mission and Evangelism:

- The prophecy's fulfillment in Christ's death and the subsequent events provided a strong basis for evangelism. The early Church could use these prophecies to demonstrate to both Jews and Gentiles that Jesus was the prophesied Messiah and that the events surrounding Him were foretold in Scripture. This prophetic fulfillment was a key component in their proclamation of the Gospel.

Chapter 9:27 Commentary:

An expository study and comprehensive commentary on Daniel 9:27 using the King James Bible.

Verse 27:

"And he shall confirm the covenant with many for one week: and in the midst of the week he shall cause the sacrifice and the oblation to cease, and for the overspreading of abominations he shall make it desolate, even until the consummation, and that determined shall be poured upon the desolate."

King James Bible's Reference:

Introduction

Daniel 9:27 concludes the prophecy of the Seventy Weeks, which has been the subject of extensive theological debate, especially concerning the identity of the one who confirms the covenant. Many interpreters view the "he" in this verse as the Antichrist, but this expository study will argue that it is, in fact, Jesus Christ who confirms the covenant, not the Antichrist.

This interpretation aligns with a Christological approach, maintaining the messianic focus throughout the passage and offering a fulfillment of prophecy that centers on Jesus' redemptive work rather than projecting a future Antichrist.

Verse Breakdown and Commentary

1. "And he shall confirm the covenant with many for one week"

- The Subject of the Sentence: "He"

The pronoun "he" refers to the subject mentioned in the previous verses. In Daniel 9:26, we read about "Messiah the Prince" being "cut off." Since the prophecy centers on the Messiah, it is consistent to interpret the "he" of verse 27 as Jesus Christ. This is supported by the flow of the text, which speaks of the Messiah's work, death, and covenant with God's people.

Confirming the Covenant:

The word "confirm" comes from the Hebrew word gabar (גָּבַר), meaning "to strengthen" or "to make firm." This implies that the covenant being referred to already existed and was not newly created. Jesus, during His ministry, confirmed the promises God made to Israel, fulfilling the Old Covenant through His teachings, His perfect obedience to the Law, and, ultimately, His sacrificial death.

Jesus Himself spoke of the "new covenant" during the Last Supper: "This cup is the new covenant in My blood, which is shed for you" (Luke 22:20, NKJV). This covenant was not a departure from God's promises to Israel but a fulfillment of them, confirmed by the Messiah.

- "With many"

The phrase "with many" refers to those who would benefit from the covenant. In the first instance, Jesus' ministry was directed toward Israel, as He said, "I was sent only to the lost sheep of Israel" (Matthew 15:24, NIV). However, through His death and resurrection, the covenant extended to the Gentiles, fulfilling God's promise to Abraham that through his seed, all nations would be blessed (Genesis 12:3).

The New Testament frequently emphasizes the "many" who are partakers of this covenant (cf. Matthew 26:28, Romans 5:15). Jesus' confirmation of the covenant was indeed for the "many," both Jew and Gentile, who would believe in Him.

- "For one week"

The "one week" refers to a period of seven years, following the prophetic model of weeks in Daniel 9. Jesus' earthly ministry lasted approximately three and a half years, and the prophecy states that "in the midst of the week" He would cause the sacrifice to cease. The remainder of the "week" could be understood as the period following Jesus' resurrection, during which the Gospel was preached to the Jews until the focus shifted to the Gentiles.

2. "And in the midst of the week he shall cause the sacrifice and the oblation to cease"

- "In the midst of the week"

This phrase indicates that something significant would occur halfway through the "week," or after three and a half years. This timing aligns perfectly with the duration of Jesus' public ministry. After about three and a half years of teaching, healing, and ministering, Jesus was "cut off" (crucified), as foretold in Daniel 9:26.

- "Cause the sacrifice and the oblation to cease"

With Jesus' death on the cross, the entire system of temple sacrifices became obsolete. His sacrifice was the final and complete atonement for sin, rendering the ongoing sacrifices under the Old Covenant unnecessary.

The Epistle to the Hebrews clarifies this truth: "But this Man, after He had offered one sacrifice for sins forever, sat down at the right hand of God" (Hebrews 10:12, NKJV). Jesus' once-for-all sacrifice on the cross caused the cessation of the sacrificial system that had been central to Jewish worship for centuries.

The "oblation" refers to the grain offerings that accompanied sacrifices in the temple. The end of the temple sacrifices and oblations was not immediately realized after Jesus' death but was symbolically demonstrated when the veil of the temple was torn in two (Matthew 27:51), signifying the end of the Old Covenant system.

3. "For the overspreading of abominations he shall make it desolate"

- "Overspreading of abominations"

The term "abominations" (shiqqutz, שִׁקּוּץ) refers to something detestable or repugnant, often associated with idolatry. The "overspreading" suggests an abundance or increase of these abominations, which would lead to desolation. This likely refers to the events surrounding the destruction of the temple in A.D. 70, when Jerusalem was laid waste by the Romans.

Jesus Himself predicted this desolation in Matthew 24:15-16, where He refers to the "abomination of desolation" spoken of by Daniel. The Roman siege and destruction of Jerusalem fulfilled this prophecy, marking the judgment upon the city for rejecting the Messiah.

- "Shall make it desolate"

The desolation of Jerusalem and the temple was a direct consequence of the Jewish leaders' rejection of Jesus. As prophesied in Daniel 9:26, the city would be destroyed by "the people of the prince who is to come," which many interpret as the Roman forces under Titus.

4. "Even until the consummation, and that determined shall be poured upon the desolate"

- "Until the consummation"

The word "consummation" refers to the completion or fulfillment of God's judgment. The period of desolation would continue until God's predetermined end, signaling His complete and final judgment.

- "That determined shall be poured upon the desolate"

God's judgment upon Jerusalem and the Jewish people for rejecting the Messiah was poured out in full measure during the destruction of the city and the temple in A.D. 70. This desolation was the result of their continued disobedience and refusal to accept the covenant confirmed by Christ.

Conclusion: Jesus, Not Antichrist

The comprehensive study of Daniel 9:27 strongly supports the interpretation that Jesus Christ is the one who confirms the covenant, not the Antichrist. The prophecy outlines Jesus' ministry, His sacrificial death, and the cessation of the Old Covenant sacrificial system. The desolation described in the passage refers to the consequences of rejecting the Messiah, culminating in the destruction of Jerusalem in A.D. 70.

This Christ-centered interpretation aligns with the broader message of the Bible, which consistently points to Jesus as the fulfillment of God's covenant promises. By interpreting Daniel 9:27 in light of the New Testament and historical events, we can see a profound and accurate fulfillment of the prophecy in the life, death, and ministry of Jesus Christ.

Daniel 9:27, though part of a prophecy given long ago, holds significant meaning for believers today. The verse, which discusses the confirmation of a covenant, the cessation of sacrifices, and the desolation caused by abominations, continues to have theological and spiritual implications. Let's explore how Daniel 9:27 applies to contemporary faith and understanding.

1. The Fulfillment of the Covenant

- Christ's New Covenant: In the modern era, Daniel 9:27 emphasizes the fulfillment of the covenant through Jesus Christ. The "he" who confirms the covenant is understood by many scholars to be Jesus, and His death established the New Covenant, which remains in effect today.

- Relevance for Believers: Christians today live under this New Covenant. Jesus' sacrifice, which ended the need for the Old Testament sacrificial system, assures believers of salvation through faith. The covenant Jesus confirmed applies to all who accept Him, and His promise of eternal life and reconciliation with God continues to be the foundation of Christian faith.

2. The Ceasing of Sacrifices

- End of the Old Sacrificial System: Daniel 9:27's reference to the cessation of sacrifices has lasting significance. Jesus' death was the ultimate and final sacrifice, rendering the animal sacrifices of the Old Testament obsolete. Hebrews 10:10-14 confirms this: "we have been sanctified through the offering of the body of Jesus Christ once for all."

- Modern Application: Today, believers do not rely on temple sacrifices to atone for sin but on the once-and-for-all sacrifice of Jesus. The cessation of sacrifices reminds Christians that Jesus' sacrifice was sufficient to cover all sin, past, present, and future. It underscores the importance of grace, faith, and forgiveness in modern Christian life.

3. Warning Against Apostasy and Abominations

- Desolation and Judgment: The "abominations" that lead to desolation in Daniel 9:27 can be seen as a warning against apostasy and idolatry. Historically, the rejection of Jesus by the Jewish leadership led to the destruction of Jerusalem and the temple in A.D. 70. Today, this serves as a cautionary reminder.

- Application for the Church: The modern Church must be vigilant against any form of spiritual compromise, idolatry, or rejection of Christ's teachings. Daniel 9:27 warns of the consequences of turning away from God and embracing ungodly practices. The desolation caused by such actions is not only historical but spiritual, affecting individuals and communities that forsake their faith.

4. Hope and the Consummation of God's Plan

- Ongoing Relevance: Daniel 9:27 speaks of desolation continuing "until the consummation" of God's plan. While much of the prophecy has already been fulfilled, Christians today still await the ultimate consummation of God's plan: the second coming of Christ, the final judgment, and the establishment of His eternal kingdom.

- Living in Expectation: The reference to "the consummation" points believers to the hope of Christ's return. Although the prophecy was fulfilled in part with Jesus' first coming and the destruction of Jerusalem, its ultimate fulfillment will occur when Christ returns. This encourages Christians to live in faith, with a sense of urgency and expectation for the future consummation of all things.

5. A Call to Faithfulness

- Confirming the Covenant in Daily Life: Daniel 9:27 applies to today as a call to embrace and live out the covenant Jesus confirmed. Christians are called to live faithfully within the terms of the New Covenant—trusting in Christ's atoning work, following His teachings, and sharing the Gospel with others.

- Spiritual Application: This prophecy also invites modern believers to recognize the importance of staying faithful to God's promises and avoiding any forms of spiritual decay. It serves as a reminder to cling to the New Covenant as the foundation for a life of obedience and worship.

Conclusion: Daniel 9:27's Application for Today

Daniel 9:27, while rooted in an ancient context, continues to have deep relevance for believers today. It points to the finished work of Jesus Christ, the ongoing call to faithfulness, and the hope of God's ultimate plan. This prophecy encourages Christians to live in the assurance of Christ's atoning work, to avoid spiritual compromise, and to anticipate the consummation of God's redemptive plan.

Today, believers can apply the lessons of Daniel 9:27 by trusting fully in Jesus' sacrifice, maintaining faithfulness to the New Covenant, and looking forward with hope to the final fulfillment of God's promises.

CHAPTER

07

THEOLOGICAL IMPLICATIONS

Messianic Prophecies and Their Fulfillment

The seventy-week prophecy in Daniel 9:24-27 is a cornerstone of messianic prophecy, providing a detailed timeline and description of events leading to the arrival of the Messiah. Understanding these prophecies and their fulfillment is crucial for appreciating the theological depth and significance of Daniel's vision.

1. Specific Predictions:

- Timing: The prophecy accurately predicts the timing of the Messiah's arrival, corresponding to the historical period of Jesus Christ's ministry. The seven weeks plus sixty-two weeks (483 years) from the decree to rebuild Jerusalem to the coming of the Anointed One align closely with the life and ministry of Jesus.

- Nature of the Messiah: The description of the Messiah being "cut off" without receiving His due, and the implications of atonement for sin, align with the crucifixion and sacrificial death of Jesus.

2. Fulfillment in Jesus Christ:

- Historical Evidence: Jesus' life, death, and resurrection fulfill the specific predictions made in the seventy weeks prophecy. This includes His role as the suffering servant (Isaiah 53), His crucifixion (Daniel 9:26), and the subsequent destruction of Jerusalem and the temple (Daniel 9:26-27).

- Confirmation of Prophecy: The detailed fulfillment of these prophecies in the person of Jesus Christ confirms the reliability and divine inspiration of biblical prophecy. It demonstrates God's sovereign control over history and His faithfulness in fulfilling His promises.

The Role of Jesus Christ in Daniel's Prophecy

Jesus Christ is central to the fulfillment of Daniel's prophecy, embodying the role of the Anointed One who brings about the six key objectives outlined in Daniel 9:24.

1. Atonement for Sin:

- Sacrificial Death: Jesus' crucifixion provided the atonement for humanity's sins, satisfying the requirements of divine justice and offering redemption. His death is the ultimate fulfillment of the sacrificial system outlined in the Old Testament.

- New Covenant: Through His death and resurrection, Jesus established the New Covenant, offering forgiveness and eternal life to all who believe in Him. This covenant is marked by the indwelling of the Holy Spirit and the transformation of believers' lives.

2. Bringing in Everlasting Righteousness:

- Righteousness Through Faith: Jesus' sacrifice and resurrection opened the way for believers to be declared righteous before God through faith. This imputed righteousness is a key component of the gospel message.

- Kingdom of God: Jesus' teachings and actions inaugurated the Kingdom of God, a present reality and future hope for believers. His second coming will fully establish this kingdom, bringing everlasting righteousness and justice.

3. Sealing Up Vision and Prophecy:

- Fulfillment of Prophecies: Jesus' life and work fulfilled numerous Old Testament prophecies, affirming the reliability of Scripture. His fulfillment of these prophecies confirms the truth of God's word and His redemptive plan.

- Revelation of God's Plan: Jesus' ministry provided a fuller revelation of God's plan for salvation, culminating in the New Testament writings that expand on the implications of His life, death, and resurrection.

4. Anointing the Most Holy Place:

- Heavenly Sanctuary: Jesus' ascension and His role as the high priest in the heavenly sanctuary (Hebrews 4:14-16) signify the ultimate anointing of the Most Holy Place. His intercession for believers assures them of continuous access to God's presence.

- Eschatological Fulfillment: The ultimate fulfillment of this aspect will occur in the New Jerusalem, where God will dwell with His people forever (Revelation 21:3).

The Implications for Eschatology

The seventy-week prophecy also has significant implications for eschatology, the study of the end times. It provides a framework for understanding future events and the ultimate fulfillment of God's redemptive plan.

1. Final Week and Future Events:

- The Antichrist: Many scholars interpret the final week as involving the rise of a future Antichrist who will confirm a covenant, break it, and set up the abomination of desolation. This period is often associated with the tribulation described in the book of Revelation.

- Second Coming of Christ: The prophecy points towards the second coming of Christ, who will return to judge the living and the dead, establish His eternal kingdom, and bring an end to all evil and suffering.

2. Hope and Assurance:

- God's Sovereignty: The fulfillment of the seventy weeks prophecy provides assurance of God's sovereignty over history and His faithfulness in keeping His promises. Believers can trust that the remaining unfulfilled aspects will come to pass according to God's perfect timing.

- Eschatological Hope: The prophecy reinforces the hope of the resurrection and the ultimate restoration of all things. It encourages believers to remain faithful, watchful, and prepared for Christ's return.

3. Interpretive Approaches:

- Preterist: This view interprets the seventy weeks as entirely fulfilled in the past, particularly in the events surrounding the life of Jesus and the destruction of Jerusalem in A.D. 70.

- Historicist: This approach sees the seventy weeks as spanning various historical periods, with the final week symbolizing ongoing or future events.

- Futurist: This perspective views the final week as yet to be fulfilled, involving a future Antichrist and the tribulation period before Christ's second coming.

- Idealist: This interpretation understands the prophecy in a more symbolic or allegorical manner, focusing on its theological and spiritual implications rather than specific historical events.

CHAPTER

08

INTERPRETATIONS OF THE 70 WEEKS

Preterist, Historicist, Futurist, and Idealist Views

The seventy-week prophecy in Daniel 9:24-27 has been interpreted through various theological lenses. Each interpretive approach offers distinct perspectives on the timing and fulfillment of the prophecy. Here, we explore the four main views: Preterist, Historicist, Futurist, and Idealist.

1. Preterist View:

   - Description: The Preterist view holds that the seventy-week prophecy was entirely fulfilled in the past, specifically during the period leading up to and including the destruction of Jerusalem in A.D. 70.

   - Key Points:

   - First Seven Weeks: Refers to the period of Jerusalem's rebuilding following the decree by Artaxerxes.

   - Sixty-Two Weeks: Spans from the completion of the rebuilding to the ministry of Jesus.

   - Final Week: Encompasses the events of Jesus' ministry, crucifixion, and the subsequent destruction of Jerusalem by the Romans.

2. Historicist View:

   - Description: The Historicist view sees the seventy weeks as spanning various historical periods, with each segment corresponding to significant events in church history.

   - Key Points:

   - First Seven Weeks: Rebuilding of Jerusalem.

   - Sixty-Two Weeks: Period leading up to the coming of Christ.

- Final Week: Represents key events in church history, often interpreted symbolically to cover long periods.

3. Futurist View:

- Description: The Futurist view interprets the final week of the prophecy as yet to be fulfilled, involving a future Antichrist and a period of tribulation before the second coming of Christ.

- Key Points:

- First Seven Weeks: Rebuilding of Jerusalem.

- Sixty-Two Weeks: Leads up to the crucifixion of Jesus.

- Final Week: Separated by a gap, with the last seven years involving a future covenant, the rise of the Antichrist, and the abomination of desolation.

4. Idealist View:

- Description: The Idealist view understands the seventy weeks prophecy in a more symbolic or allegorical manner, focusing on its theological and spiritual implications rather than specific historical events.

- Key Points:

- Symbolic Representation: The prophecy represents the ongoing struggle between good and evil, the work of Christ, and the ultimate triumph of God's kingdom.

- Spiritual Fulfillment: Emphasizes the spiritual truths and principles illustrated by the prophecy rather than pinpointing exact historical events.

Strengths and Weaknesses of Each Interpretation

1. Preterist View:

- Strengths:

- Historical Consistency: Aligns well with known historical events and the destruction of Jerusalem in A.D. 70.

- Immediate Fulfillment: Offers a coherent narrative for early Christians and the context of Jesus' prophecy.

- Weaknesses:

- Future Prophetic Elements: May struggle to account for future-oriented aspects of the prophecy and eschatological hope.

- Limited Scope: Can be seen as too narrowly focused on the past, potentially neglecting broader theological implications.

2. Historicist View:

- Strengths:

- Comprehensive Timeline: Attempts to provide a continuous historical narrative linking biblical prophecy with church history.

- Symbolic Depth: Offers rich symbolic interpretations that can be spiritually enriching.

- Weaknesses:

- Complexity and Subjectivity: The historical application can be complex and sometimes subjective, leading to varied interpretations.

- Lack of Consensus: Historical interpretations often lack a clear consensus among scholars.

3. Futurist View:

- Strengths:

- Clarity on Eschatology: Provides a clear and distinct framework for understanding future events and the second coming of Christ.

- Alignment with Revelation: Consistent with the eschatological themes in the book of Revelation and other prophetic texts.

- Weaknesses:

- Gap Theory: The concept of a gap between the sixty-ninth and seventieth week can be seen as speculative and lacks explicit biblical support.

- Overemphasis on Future: May neglect the historical and immediate fulfillment aspects of the prophecy.

4. Idealist View:

- Strengths:

- Theological and Spiritual Insight: Focuses on the enduring spiritual truths and theological implications of the prophecy.

- Timeless Relevance: Emphasizes the perpetual relevance of the prophecy for all believers.

- Weaknesses:

- Lack of Historical Specificity: May be criticized for not addressing the concrete historical fulfillments of the prophecy.

- Ambiguity: This can be seen as too abstract, lacking the concrete details that other interpretations provide.

The Consensus Among Scholars

While there is no unanimous consensus among scholars regarding the interpretation of the seventy weeks prophecy, certain aspects are widely accepted:

1. Historical Context: Most scholars agree on the historical context of the prophecy, including the decrees to rebuild Jerusalem and the period leading up to the coming of Jesus Christ.

2. Messianic Fulfillment: There is general consensus that the prophecy points to the coming of the Messiah, with Jesus Christ fulfilling many aspects of the prophecy, particularly the "cutting off" of the Anointed One.

3. Destruction of Jerusalem: The prophecy's prediction of the destruction of Jerusalem and the temple is widely recognized as having been fulfilled in A.D. 70 by the Romans.

4. Varied Interpretations: Scholars acknowledge the validity of different interpretive frameworks (Preterist, Historicist, Futurist, Idealist), each contributing unique insights into understanding the prophecy's complexity and richness.

09

MODERN RELEVANCE

Lessons for Today's Believers

The seventy-week prophecy in Daniel 9:24-27 holds significant lessons for contemporary believers. Its themes of divine sovereignty, redemption, and fulfillment of promises provide a foundation for understanding God's ongoing work in history and our lives.

1. Faithfulness in Adversity:

- Daniel's Example: Daniel's unwavering faith and commitment to God during his time in Babylon serve as an inspiring model for believers today. Despite living in a foreign and often hostile environment, Daniel remained steadfast in his devotion, prayer, and obedience.

- Application: In modern times, believers are often faced with challenges and pressures that can test their faith. Daniel's example encourages us to remain faithful and trust in God's providence, even in difficult circumstances.

2. Hope in God's Promises:

- Fulfillment of Prophecy: The detailed fulfillment of the seventy weeks prophecy in the life, death, and resurrection of Jesus Christ demonstrates God's faithfulness to His promises. This fulfillment assures us that God's word is true and reliable.

- Application: Believers can have hope and confidence in God's promises for the future, including the promise of eternal life, the return of Christ, and the establishment of His kingdom. This hope provides strength and encouragement in our daily walk with God.

3. Intercessory Prayer:

- Daniel's Prayer: Daniel's heartfelt prayer of confession and supplication in Daniel 9:1-19 highlights the power and importance of intercessory prayer. His prayer was sincere, humble, and aligned with God's will.

- Application: Today, believers are called to pray for others, intercede for their communities, and seek God's guidance and intervention. Intercessory prayer is a powerful tool for spiritual growth and for bringing about God's purposes in our world.

Prophecy and Faith

Understanding biblical prophecy is vital for strengthening our faith and deepening our relationship with God. Prophecies like the seventy weeks in Daniel provide a roadmap of God's redemptive plan and His control over history.

1. Reaffirmation of God's Sovereignty:

- Divine Control: The precise fulfillment of the seventy-week prophecy reaffirms that God is in control of history. He orchestrates events according to His divine plan, ensuring that His purposes are accomplished.

- Application: Believers can trust in God's sovereignty, knowing that He is in control of their lives and the broader events of history. This trust brings peace and assurance, especially in times of uncertainty.

2. Strengthening of Faith:

- Evidence of Fulfillment: The accurate fulfillment of prophecy serves as evidence of the truthfulness and reliability of Scripture. It strengthens our faith in God's word and His promises.

- Application: Studying biblical prophecies and their fulfillments can deepen our faith and encourage us to rely more fully on God's word. It reminds us that God is faithful and that His promises are sure.

3. Encouragement for Perseverance:

- Future Hope: Prophecies about the end times and the second coming of Christ provide hope and motivation for believers to persevere in their faith.

- Application: The knowledge that Christ will return and establish His kingdom encourages us to remain faithful, live righteously, and share the gospel with others. It provides a future-oriented perspective that helps us endure present challenges.

The Importance of Understanding Biblical Prophecies

Biblical prophecies are not merely historical curiosities; they are integral to our understanding of God's nature, His plans, and our place within His story.

1. Insight into God's Plan:

- Comprehensive Understanding: Prophecies like the seventy weeks provide a comprehensive view of God's redemptive plan, from the coming of the Messiah to the ultimate restoration of all things.

- Application: Understanding these prophecies helps us see the big picture of God's work in history and our role within it. It encourages us to align our lives with His purposes and live with a sense of divine mission.

2. Theological Foundation:

- Doctrinal Clarity: Prophecies contribute to our theological understanding of key doctrines such as the atonement, the second coming of Christ, and the final judgment.

- Application: A sound understanding of biblical prophecies helps us develop a robust theology that informs our beliefs and practices. It equips us to articulate our faith and engage in meaningful theological discussions.

3. Preparation and Vigilance:

- Eschatological Awareness: Prophecies about the end times encourage believers to be watchful, prepared, and discerning about the signs of the times.

- Application: Understanding eschatological prophecies helps us live with a sense of readiness for Christ's return. It prompts us to cultivate a life of holiness, evangelism, and service, knowing that our time is limited and significant.

CHAPTER

10

RECAP OF KEY POINTS

Recap of Key Points

Throughout this book, we have explored the profound and intricate prophecy of the seventy weeks found in Daniel 9:24-27. This prophecy, delivered by the angel Gabriel to Daniel, outlines God's redemptive timeline for Israel and the world, culminating in the coming of the Messiah and the ultimate restoration of all things. Here are the key points we have covered:

1. The Context of Daniel's Prophecy:

- The Babylonian exile and Daniel's role in Babylon.

- Daniel's prayer and confession, leading to Gabriel's revelation.

2. Understanding Biblical Prophecy:

- The nature and importance of prophetic literature in the Bible.

- The use of symbolism and numbers in prophecy.

- The concept of "weeks" as periods of seven years in the biblical context.

3. The Seventy Weeks Explained (Daniel 9:24):

- Analysis of the seventy weeks and their purpose.

- The six objectives: finishing transgression, putting an end to sin, atoning for wickedness, bringing in everlasting righteousness, sealing up vision and prophecy, and anointing the Most Holy Place.

4. The First Seven Weeks (Daniel 9:25):

- Historical fulfillment with the rebuilding of Jerusalem.

- The roles of Nehemiah and Ezra in the restoration process.

5. The Sixty-Two Weeks (Daniel 9:25):

- Analysis of the sixty-two weeks and historical events.

- The coming of the Anointed One, Jesus Christ, and the fulfillment of messianic prophecies.

6. The Final Week (Daniel 9:26-27):

- The cutting off of the Anointed One (Jesus' crucifixion).

- The destruction of Jerusalem and the temple by the Romans.

- The future implications of the covenant and the abomination of desolation.

7. Theological Implications:

- The fulfillment of messianic prophecies in Jesus Christ.

- The significance of eschatology and the future fulfillment of God's plan.

8. Interpretations of the 70 Weeks:

- Overview of Preterist, Historicist, Futurist, and Idealist views.

- Strengths and weaknesses of each interpretation.

- Consensus among scholars on key aspects of the prophecy.

9. Modern Relevance:

- Lessons for today's believers from Daniel's example and the prophecy's fulfillment.

- The role of prophecy in strengthening faith.

- The importance of understanding biblical prophecies for theological clarity and preparedness.

The Hope and Assurance in God's Plan

The seventy-week prophecy provides believers with profound hope and assurance in God's sovereign plan. Through this prophecy, we see the meticulous fulfillment of God's promises and His unwavering faithfulness. Key takeaways include:

1. God's Sovereignty:

- The detailed and precise fulfillment of the prophecy demonstrates that God is in control of history. He orchestrates events according to His divine plan, ensuring that His purposes are accomplished.

2. The Fulfillment of Promises:

- The arrival of the Anointed One, Jesus Christ, and His sacrificial death for the atonement of sins fulfill God's redemptive promises. This fulfillment assures us of the reliability and truth of Scripture.

3. Hope for the Future:

- The prophecy not only addresses past and present events but also points to future fulfillment. The anticipation of Christ's second coming and the establishment of His eternal kingdom provide hope and motivation for believers to persevere in their faith.

4. Assurance in Trials:

- Just as Daniel remained faithful in the face of adversity, believers today can draw strength and assurance from God's promises. The prophecy encourages us to remain steadfast, knowing that God's plan will ultimately prevail.

Encouragement for Further Study

The study of biblical prophecy, especially complex and significant prophecies like the seventy weeks, requires diligent study and a heart open to God's guidance. Here are some encouragements for further study:

1. Deepen Your Understanding:

- Engage with biblical commentaries, theological works, and scholarly articles that explore the seventy weeks prophecy and related eschatological themes. This will provide a deeper and more nuanced understanding of the text.

2. Explore Related Prophecies:

- Study other prophetic books in the Old and New Testaments, such as Isaiah, Ezekiel, Zechariah, and Revelation. This will help you see the broader context of biblical prophecy and how they interconnect.

3. Reflect and Pray:

- Spend time in reflection and prayer, asking God to reveal His truths to you through His word. Let the study of prophecy strengthen your faith and draw you closer to God.

4. Join a Study Group:

- Consider joining a Bible study group or a theological class that focuses on biblical prophecy. Engaging with others in discussion and study can provide new insights and deepen your understanding.

5. Apply the Lessons:

- Apply the lessons learned from the study of Daniel's prophecy to your daily life. Let the themes of faithfulness, hope, and assurance guide your walk with God and influence your interactions with others.

70 WEEKS EXPLAINATIONS

The Seventy Weeks Prophecy, found in Daniel 9:24-27, is one of the most significant and complex prophetic passages in the Bible. It outlines God's plan for Israel and the coming of the Messiah. The prophecy is known for its detailed timeline of "weeks" and its prediction of key events in redemptive history.

Context of the Prophecy

The prophecy is given to Daniel while he is praying and confessing the sins of Israel during the Babylonian Exile. Daniel had been studying the writings of Jeremiah, which predicted a 70-year exile for Israel (Jeremiah 25:11-12). Gabriel, the angel, appears to Daniel and delivers this prophecy, revealing a broader timeframe of 70 "weeks" (literally, "sevens"), which extend far beyond the 70-year exile and predict the coming of the Messiah and future events.

The Structure of the Seventy Weeks

The prophecy divides the 70 weeks into three distinct periods:

1. Seven Weeks (49 years)
2. Sixty-two Weeks (434 years)
3. One Week (7 years)

Together, these total 70 weeks, or 490 years (since each "week" represents seven years).

Verse-by-Verse Breakdown

1. Daniel 9:24 – The Purpose of the Seventy Weeks

"Seventy weeks are determined for your people and for your holy city, to finish the transgression, to make an end of sins, to make reconciliation for iniquity, to bring in everlasting righteousness, to seal up vision and prophecy, and to anoint the Most Holy." (NKJV)

This verse outlines the six key purposes of the Seventy Weeks:

1. Finish the transgression: Bringing an end to Israel's rebellion against God.

2. Make an end of sins: This points to dealing with sin, which was accomplished by Jesus' atonement on the cross.

3. Make reconciliation for iniquity: Jesus' death brought reconciliation between God and humanity.

4. Bring in everlasting righteousness: Through Jesus' reign and the establishment of His eternal kingdom.

5. Seal up vision and prophecy: Fulfillment of prophecies regarding Israel and the Messiah.

6. Anoint the Most Holy: Refers to the consecration of the holy place, often seen as either the heavenly sanctuary or Jesus as the anointed one.

2. Daniel 9:25 – The First 69 Weeks (Seven Weeks + Sixty-Two Weeks)

"Know therefore and understand, that from the going forth of the command to restore and build Jerusalem until Messiah the Prince, there shall be seven weeks and sixty-two weeks; the street shall be built again, and the wall, even in troublesome times." (NKJV)

- Seven Weeks (49 years):

The prophecy begins with a decree to restore and rebuild Jerusalem. Historically, this decree is associated with Artaxerxes I, who issued the command to Nehemiah to rebuild Jerusalem's walls around 445 B.C. (Nehemiah 2:1-8). The "seven weeks" refer to the 49 years during which Jerusalem was rebuilt, despite opposition and difficult conditions.

- Sixty-two Weeks (434 years):

After the first seven weeks, there is a period of 62 weeks (434 years) that leads up to the coming of the "Messiah the Prince." This period covers the time from the completion of Jerusalem's rebuilding until the arrival of Jesus Christ. This timeline places the end of the 62 weeks near the time of Jesus' public ministry.

3. Daniel 9:26 – The Messiah Is "Cut Off" and the Destruction of Jerusalem

"And after the sixty-two weeks Messiah shall be cut off, but not for Himself; and the people of the prince who is to come shall destroy the city and the sanctuary. The end of it shall be with a flood, and till the end of the war desolations are determined." (NKJV)

- Messiah Shall Be Cut Off:

After the 69 weeks (7 + 62 = 69, or 483 years), the Messiah is "cut off," which is widely interpreted as Jesus' crucifixion. Jesus was "cut off" from life, but not for Himself—He died for the sins of others.

- The Destruction of the City and the Sanctuary:

After the Messiah is cut off, "the people of the prince who is to come" will destroy Jerusalem and the temple. This was fulfilled in A.D. 70 when the Roman armies under Titus destroyed Jerusalem and the second temple. The "prince" here is often understood as a reference to the Roman general (and later emperor) Titus.

4. Daniel 9:27 – The Final Week

"Then he shall confirm a covenant with many for one week; but in the middle of the week he shall bring an end to sacrifice and offering. And on the wing of abominations shall be one who makes desolate, even until the consummation, which is determined, is poured out on the desolate." (NKJV)

- He Shall Confirm a Covenant:

This "one week" (the final seven-year period) has been interpreted in different ways. Some believe it refers to the Antichrist making a covenant with Israel, but an alternate and convincing interpretation is that "he" refers to Jesus, who confirmed the New Covenant with many (cf. Matthew 26:28). Jesus' ministry lasted for approximately three and a half years, which aligns with "the middle of the week."

- Bring an End to Sacrifice and Offering:

Jesus' sacrificial death on the cross put an end to the need for temple sacrifices (Hebrews 10:12-14). This cessation of sacrifices corresponds to the "middle of the week," as Jesus' ministry was cut short after three and a half years.

- Abomination of Desolation:

The latter part of the verse refers to desolation, often interpreted as the destruction of Jerusalem in A.D. 70. Jesus referenced this event in Matthew 24:15, warning of the coming destruction by the Roman armies.

Interpretation of the Final Week

The final "week" is often seen as a period of seven years, with the first half being fulfilled by Jesus' ministry and crucifixion. The remaining three and a half years are sometimes viewed symbolically, representing the continued unfolding of God's plan, potentially pointing to the future and the second coming of Christ.

Key Points to Understand

1. Seventy Weeks Equals 490 Years:

Each "week" in this prophecy is interpreted as a period of seven years. Therefore, 70 weeks equals 490 years.

2. Historical and Prophetic Fulfillment:

The first 69 weeks (483 years) are seen as historically fulfilled, culminating in the arrival of Jesus and His crucifixion. The destruction of Jerusalem in A.D. 70 fulfills the desolation predicted in the prophecy.

3. Messiah-Centered Fulfillment:

The prophecy centers on Jesus, the Messiah. He is the one who confirms the covenant and brings an end to the Old Testament sacrificial system through His death.

4. The Final Week:

Interpretations vary regarding the final "week." Some see a future fulfillment involving the Antichrist, while others view the "week" as completed in Christ's first coming, with the final consummation yet to come.

Modern Relevance

For Christians, the Seventy Weeks prophecy reveals the precision of God's plan for salvation through Jesus Christ. It also encourages believers to remain faithful, understanding that God's timeline is perfect, and the prophecy speaks both to the past and the future.

The prophecy continues to provide hope for the ultimate fulfillment of God's promises, pointing toward the second coming of Christ and the establishment of His eternal kingdom.

The Seventy Weeks Prophecy of Daniel (Daniel 9:24-27) has significant connections to the end times, as it outlines both the first coming of the Messiah and events that many interpret as foreshadowing the future tribulation and return of Christ. Let's explore how this prophecy relates to the end times, focusing particularly on the final or 70th week.

The Structure of the Seventy Weeks Prophecy

The prophecy is divided into three parts:

1. Seven weeks (49 years): This period likely refers to the rebuilding of Jerusalem after the decree of Artaxerxes to Nehemiah in 445 B.C.

2. Sixty-two weeks (434 years): This period leads up to the time of the Messiah, culminating in His arrival and crucifixion. After the 69th week (7 + 62 = 69), the Messiah is "cut off" (a reference to Jesus' crucifixion).

3. One final week (7 years): This is often seen as a future period, sometimes called the 70th week, and is connected to end-times events.

End Times and the Final Week:

The connection to the end times centers on the final, 70th week. Many interpreters believe that the events of this last week are yet to be fulfilled and relate to the tribulation and the return of Christ.

1. The Gap Between the 69th and 70th Week

- After the 69th week (when the Messiah is cut off), the prophecy transitions to future events. The prophecy mentions the destruction of Jerusalem (which occurred in A.D. 70) but then moves forward to describe a final seven-year period.

- Many scholars believe there is a gap between the 69th and 70th week—essentially the "Church Age," which began after Jesus' death and resurrection and continues until the end times. This gap explains why the 70th week is often interpreted as a future event.

2. The Final Week (Seven Years) and the End Times

- The final "week" or seven-year period is frequently connected with the tribulation, a key event in end-times prophecy. This period is often divided into two halves: three and a half years of relative peace, followed by three and a half years of intense tribulation.

- This final seven-year period is described in more detail in the Book of Revelation and is believed to include key events such as the rise of the Antichrist, a peace agreement with Israel, and the eventual betrayal of that agreement.

3. The Covenant and the Antichrist (Alternate View)

- Daniel 9:27 mentions that "he shall confirm a covenant with many for one week." Many futurist interpreters believe that the "he" in this verse refers to the Antichrist, who will make a seven-year peace agreement with Israel. This peace covenant will appear to bring stability to the region, but in the middle of the seven-year period (after three and a half years), the Antichrist will break the covenant.

- This breaking of the covenant will result in the Abomination of Desolation, where the Antichrist desecrates the temple (referenced in Daniel 9:27 and by Jesus in Matthew 24:15). This abomination marks the beginning of intense persecution and tribulation during the second half of the final week.

4. The Abomination of Desolation

- The Abomination of Desolation is a pivotal event tied to the end times. Jesus referred to it in His discourse about the last days (Matthew 24:15-16), warning that when this event occurs, those in Judea should flee to the mountains.

- According to this view, the Abomination of Desolation will happen midway through the 70th week when the Antichrist desecrates the Jewish temple by setting up an image of himself to be worshiped. This will initiate the Great Tribulation, the second half of the 70th week.

5. The Great Tribulation

- The second half of the final seven-year period is referred to as the Great Tribulation, a time of unparalleled suffering and persecution (Matthew 24:21). During this period, the Antichrist will exert global control, and God's judgments will be poured out on the earth (as seen in the seals, trumpets, and bowl judgments of Revelation).

- This tribulation period is often identified as three and a half years, aligning with Daniel's description of the final "half of the week."

6. The Return of Christ and the End of the 70th Week

- At the end of the 70th week, Jesus will return to defeat the Antichrist and establish His millennial kingdom (Revelation 19:11-21). The Second Coming of Christ is the ultimate event that ends the tribulation and brings about the fulfillment of God's promises, including the restoration of Israel and the establishment of everlasting righteousness (Daniel 9:24).

- This return brings to completion the final week of Daniel's prophecy, culminating in the consummation of all things. God's plan for redemption, as laid out in the Seventy Weeks Prophecy, will be fully realized when Christ returns and judges the nations.

Summary of End-Times Events Connected to the Seventy Weeks

- The Gap: Between the 69th and 70th week is the Church Age, which continues until the end times.

- The 70th Week: The final seven years (the last "week") is connected to the future tribulation, divided into two halves: the first half being relative peace, the second half marked by great tribulation.

- The Covenant with Many: The Antichrist will make and break a covenant with Israel during this final week.

- The Abomination of Desolation: Midway through the week, the Antichrist will desecrate the temple, leading to intense persecution.

- The Great Tribulation: The second half of the week is a period of great suffering, with God's judgments and the Antichrist's oppression.

- The Return of Christ: The prophecy ends with the return of Jesus, the defeat of the Antichrist, and the establishment of God's eternal kingdom.

Different Interpretive Views

There are varying interpretations of how Daniel's Seventy Weeks relate to the end times, especially the role of the 70th week:

1. Futurist View: This is the most common interpretation, particularly in dispensational theology. It sees the final week as a future seven-year tribulation period that culminates in the Second Coming of Christ.

2. Preterist View: Some preterists believe that the 70th week was fully fulfilled in the first century, particularly with the destruction of Jerusalem in A.D. 70, and that the events do not refer to the distant future.

3. Historicist View: Historicists often see the 70th week as being symbolic, representing a longer period of history, rather than a literal seven years.

4. Christ-Centered Interpretation: Another view is that the "he" who confirms the covenant in Daniel 9:27 is Jesus, who confirmed the New Covenant with His death,

rendering the 70th week as having already been fulfilled in Christ's first coming, with the final fulfillment at His return.

Conclusion: How the Seventy Weeks Relate to the End Times

The Seventy Weeks Prophecy, especially the final or 70th week, is closely linked to the end times in many eschatological interpretations. While the first 69 weeks are generally understood to have been fulfilled in the time leading up to the crucifixion of Christ, the 70th week is often seen as a future period of tribulation that will culminate in the return of Christ. This prophecy gives insight into the timeline and major events of the end times, including the rise of the Antichrist, the tribulation, and the final establishment of God's kingdom on earth.

CHAPTER

12

WHAT HAPPENS AFTER THE 70 WEEKS?

After the Seventy Weeks prophecy in Daniel 9:24-27, the timeline of God's redemptive plan continues, culminating in the final establishment of God's kingdom. The Seventy Weeks prophecy, particularly the final or 70th week, leads into a series of eschatological events that are often associated with the "end times." Here's what is believed to happen after the Seventy Weeks, depending on the interpretation.

1. End of the 70th Week

The final week (the 70th week) of the Seventy Weeks prophecy is often seen as the climactic period of the end times, marking the final phase of human history before Christ's second coming. After this week, several key events are believed to unfold:

A. The Second Coming of Christ

- Many interpreters of prophecy, especially those from a futurist or dispensational perspective, believe that after the 70th week, Jesus Christ will return to earth to defeat the Antichrist, end the tribulation, and establish His millennial kingdom.

- Revelation 19:11-21 describes Jesus' return as a conquering King, where He will defeat the forces of evil, including the Antichrist and his armies.

- This marks the conclusion of the 70th week and the ushering in of a new era in God's redemptive plan.

B. The Millennial Reign of Christ (Revelation 20:1-6)

- Following the end of the 70th week, many interpretations suggest that Jesus will establish a 1,000-year reign on earth, often called the Millennial Kingdom. This period is characterized by peace, righteousness, and the fulfillment of God's promises to Israel.

- During this time, Jesus will rule from Jerusalem, and Satan will be bound in the abyss to prevent him from deceiving the nations.

- This period is seen as a time when Christ will restore justice and righteousness, fulfilling the promises made to Israel and the church.

C. The Final Defeat of Satan and the Last Judgment

- At the end of the millennium, Satan will be released for a short time to deceive the nations one last time (Revelation 20:7-10). This leads to a final battle, where Satan and his followers will be decisively defeated.

- After Satan's defeat, the Great White Throne Judgment will occur (Revelation 20:11-15). At this judgment, all the dead will be raised, and those whose names are not found in the Book of Life will be cast into the lake of fire. This marks the final judgment of all humanity.

D. The New Heavens and New Earth

- After the final judgment, the New Heavens and the New Earth will be established (Revelation 21:1-5). God will create a new, perfect world where there will be no more sin, suffering, or death. This is the ultimate consummation of God's redemptive plan.

- The New Jerusalem, the holy city, will descend from heaven, and God will dwell with His people in perfect communion. This eternal state is marked by the complete fulfillment of all prophecies and the restoration of all things.

2. Interpretive Views of What Happens After the Seventy Weeks

The events following the Seventy Weeks prophecy are understood differently based on various eschatological viewpoints:

A. Futurist/Dispensational View

- After the 70th week: The 70th week is viewed as the seven-year tribulation period, and its conclusion brings about the second coming of Christ, the defeat of the Antichrist, and the establishment of the Millennial Kingdom.

- Millennium: After the 70th week, Christ will reign for 1,000 years, bringing peace, justice, and righteousness to the earth.

- Eternal State: After the millennial reign, Satan is defeated, the final judgment takes place, and the new heavens and new earth are established for eternity.

B. Preterist View

- After the 70th week: Some preterists believe that the 70th week was fulfilled in the first century, particularly with the destruction of Jerusalem in A.D. 70. In this view, much of what is described in the prophecy and related passages is seen as symbolic and already fulfilled in the past.

- End of History: Preterists often see the final events of history (such as the second coming and new heavens and earth) as future events, but they interpret much of Daniel's prophecy as already fulfilled in the early church.

C. Historicist View

- After the 70th week: In this view, the events of the 70th week may be seen as stretched over a long period of church history, and after this period, the return of Christ is anticipated.

- Eternal Kingdom: Historicists often emphasize the unfolding of God's kingdom throughout history and the eventual establishment of the eternal state after the final judgment.

D. Christ-Centered Interpretation

- After the 70th week: For those who see Jesus as the one who confirmed the covenant during the 70th week, the prophecy is largely fulfilled by His death and resurrection. Afterward, the focus shifts to the continued spread of the Gospel and the eventual return of Christ.

- Eschatology: After the spread of the Gospel through the church age, the return of Christ is seen as the final act in God's redemptive plan, bringing about the new creation and the eternal state.

3. Final Fulfillment of the Seventy Weeks' Purpose

The prophecy in Daniel 9:24 outlines six purposes of the Seventy Weeks, and the final fulfillment of these purposes takes place after the 70th week, particularly with the return of Christ and the establishment of His eternal kingdom. These purposes include:

- Finishing transgression: The end of rebellion against God, fully realized when sin is eradicated in the new heavens and new earth.

- Making an end of sins: The final defeat of sin and death, accomplished through Christ and completed in the eternal state.

- Making reconciliation for iniquity: Jesus' atoning sacrifice continues to be applied to believers, but its full realization will come at the end of the age when all things are reconciled to God.

- Bringing in everlasting righteousness: The kingdom of Christ brings everlasting righteousness, especially during the millennium and continuing into the eternal state.

- Sealing up vision and prophecy: The full completion of all prophecies is realized in the end times, as God's plan comes to fruition.

- Anointing the Most Holy: This may refer to the establishment of the new creation, where God dwells with His people in the New Jerusalem.

After the Seventy Weeks, particularly the 70th week, the focus of prophecy moves toward the final stages of God's redemptive plan. This includes the second coming of Christ, the defeat of evil, the establishment of His millennial kingdom, the final judgment, and the creation of the new heavens and the new earth. Ultimately, the Seventy Weeks prophecy points to the culmination of God's promises and the restoration of all things, where God's people will live with Him in eternal peace and righteousness.

The Millennial Kingdom refers to the 1,000-year reign of Jesus Christ on earth, as described in Revelation 20:1-6. This period is a central concept in premillennial eschatology, which teaches that Christ will return to earth before this thousand-year reign to establish His kingdom. The Millennial Kingdom is seen as a time of peace, righteousness, and fulfillment of God's promises to Israel and the church. Let's break down the key aspects of the Millennial Kingdom.

1. Biblical Basis for the Millennial Kingdom

The primary passage describing the Millennial Kingdom is found in Revelation 20:1-6, which details Satan being bound for 1,000 years and Christ reigning with His saints during this time:

> "Then I saw an angel coming down from heaven, holding in his hand the key to the bottomless pit and a great chain. And he seized the dragon, that ancient serpent, who is the devil and Satan, and bound him for a thousand years, and threw him into the pit, and shut it and sealed it over him, so that he might not deceive the nations any longer,

until the thousand years were ended." (Revelation 20:1-3, ESV)

During this period, Satan is bound and unable to deceive the nations, and Christ reigns as King with resurrected believers who will have authority in His kingdom.

2. Key Features of the Millennial Kingdom

A. Jesus Christ Reigns as King

- Literal Reign of Christ: The Millennial Kingdom involves the literal reign of Jesus on earth. He will rule from Jerusalem as the righteous King (Zechariah 14:9). Many prophecies in the Old Testament, particularly in the books of Isaiah, Zechariah, and Ezekiel, speak of a future reign of the Messiah over a restored Israel and the world.

- Fulfillment of Prophecies: This reign fulfills prophecies about the coming of the Messiah as a King who rules in justice, peace, and righteousness (e.g., Isaiah 9:6-7; Isaiah 11:1-10).

B. The Binding of Satan

- Satan's Imprisonment: During the 1,000 years, Satan is bound in the abyss, meaning he can no longer deceive the nations or tempt humanity (Revelation 20:1-3). His influence is temporarily removed, which allows for peace and righteousness to flourish.

- No More Deception: The absence of satanic deception during the Millennial Kingdom marks a significant difference from the current age, where Satan's influence is evident in the world.

C. Peace and Righteousness

- A Time of Peace: The Millennial Kingdom is characterized by global peace. The curse of war and violence is lifted, and nations live in harmony. Isaiah 2:4

describes a time when nations "shall beat their swords into plowshares" and "shall not learn war anymore."

- Justice and Righteousness: The reign of Christ brings perfect justice and righteousness. Under His rule, there will be no corruption, oppression, or injustice. The reign of the Messiah ensures that the poor and the oppressed are cared for (Isaiah 11:4).

- Harmony in Creation: During this period, even the natural world is transformed, and there is harmony between animals and humans (Isaiah 11:6-9). The curse placed on creation at the fall of Adam is partially lifted, and creation experiences a renewal.

D. The Resurrection and Reign of Believers

- The First Resurrection: Revelation 20:4-6 describes the resurrection of believers who reign with Christ during the Millennium. This includes those who were martyred for their faith, as well as faithful Christians who are part of the first resurrection.

- Ruling with Christ: Believers who are resurrected in the first resurrection will reign alongside Christ as rulers in His kingdom. This fulfills promises made in the New Testament, where believers are said to inherit the kingdom and reign with Christ (2 Timothy 2:12; Revelation 5:10).

E. Israel's Restoration

- Fulfillment of Promises to Israel: The Millennial Kingdom is seen as the fulfillment of God's promises to the nation of Israel, particularly the promises made to Abraham, Isaac, Jacob, and David. Many Old Testament prophecies speak of a future time when Israel will be restored to its land, experience spiritual renewal, and live under the reign of the Messiah (e.g., Ezekiel 37, Zechariah 14, Jeremiah 31:31-34).

- Restored Jerusalem: Jerusalem will be the center of global worship and governance, and the temple will be rebuilt as a place of worship (Ezekiel 40-48). All nations will come to Jerusalem to worship the Lord (Isaiah 2:2-3; Zechariah 14:16).

3. Who Will Be in the Millennial Kingdom?

- Resurrected Saints: Believers who have been resurrected in the first resurrection (described in Revelation 20:4-6) will reign with Christ during the Millennium. This includes both Old Testament saints and New Testament believers.

- Surviving Tribulation Saints: There will also be people who survive the tribulation period and enter the Millennial Kingdom in their natural bodies. These people will repopulate the earth during the Millennium.

- The Nations: The nations that remain after the tribulation will be subject to Christ's rule. Some interpretations suggest that there will be a distinction between Israel and the Gentile nations, with Israel playing a central role in the kingdom.

4. Purpose of the Millennial Kingdom

A. Fulfillment of God's Promises

- The Millennial Kingdom fulfills the promises made to Israel and the church. It is a time when God's covenant promises are fully realized, particularly the land, seed, and blessing promised to Abraham and his descendants.

- The kingdom also fulfills the Davidic Covenant, where God promised that a descendant of David would rule on his throne forever (2 Samuel 7:12-16).

B. Demonstration of God's Righteousness

- The Millennial Kingdom demonstrates the righteousness of God's rule over the earth. Christ will establish a reign of justice, peace, and holiness, showing what the world could be like when under God's direct authority.

- It is also a period of testing for humanity, showing that even in a perfect environment, with Christ reigning and Satan bound, some people will still rebel against God (Revelation 20:7-10).

5. The End of the Millennium

A. The Release of Satan

- After the 1,000 years, Satan will be released from his prison for a short time (Revelation 20:7). He will deceive the nations once more, gathering them for a final rebellion against Christ. This rebellion is often referred to as the Battle of Gog and Magog.

- The rebellion will be swiftly crushed by God, and Satan will be thrown into the lake of fire, where he will be tormented forever (Revelation 20:10).

B. The Great White Throne Judgment

- After the final rebellion, the Great White Throne Judgment will take place (Revelation 20:11-15). At this judgment, all the dead who were not part of the first resurrection will be raised and judged according to their works. Those whose names are not found in the Book of Life will be cast into the lake of fire, which is the second death.

- This judgment marks the final defeat of sin and death.

C. The New Heavens and New Earth

- Following the Millennial Kingdom, God will create a new heaven and a new earth (Revelation 21:1-5). This is the final eternal state, where God dwells with His people in perfect peace and righteousness forever.

- The New Jerusalem will descend from heaven, and all believers will enjoy eternal life in the presence of God, free from sin, suffering, and death.

The Millennial Kingdom is a unique period in redemptive history where Jesus Christ reigns as King over the earth for 1,000 years. It is characterized by peace, righteousness, and the fulfillment of God's promises to Israel and the church. During this time, Satan is bound, and Christ's reign brings global peace and justice. After the Millennium, Satan is released for a brief rebellion, which is quickly crushed, followed by the final judgment and the creation of the new heavens and new earth.

For many Christians, the Millennial Kingdom represents a foretaste of the eternal kingdom of God, where Christ's rule will be fully established, and His people will experience the blessings of His reign forever.

After the Millennium, Israel's role transitions into the eternal state alongside the rest of redeemed humanity in God's kingdom. This shift comes after the final events of the Millennium, such as the release of Satan, the final rebellion, the Great White Throne Judgment, and the creation of the new heavens and new earth. While the Bible does not specifically highlight Israel as a distinct nation in the eternal state, it does describe how God's promises to Israel, especially through covenants, are fulfilled and completed in the larger framework of God's kingdom. Here's a breakdown of Israel's role and how it fits into the eternal plan:

1. Fulfillment of God's Promises to Israel

- Covenant Promises Fulfilled: The covenants God made with Israel (e.g., the Abrahamic, Mosaic, and Davidic Covenants) are central to understanding Israel's role. During the Millennium, many of these promises—such as

Israel's restoration to the land and the reign of a Davidic king (Jesus)—are fully realized. By the time the eternal state begins, these promises will have been fulfilled, particularly those related to the land and the Davidic throne.

- The Eternal Throne of David: One of the key promises to Israel was that a descendant of David would reign forever (2 Samuel 7:16). In the Millennium, this promise is fulfilled through Christ, who reigns over the earth. After the Millennium, Jesus continues to reign in the eternal kingdom. While His reign extends beyond Israel to encompass the entire new creation, the fulfillment of the Davidic Covenant demonstrates God's faithfulness to Israel.

- Blessing to All Nations: The promise to Abraham that "in your seed all the nations of the earth shall be blessed" (Genesis 22:18) reaches its full realization in the eternal state. Through Jesus, a descendant of Abraham, this blessing extends to both Israel and the Gentiles, forming one people of God.

2. Israel as Part of God's People in the Eternal State

- Unified People of God: In the eternal state, the distinction between Israel and the church fades, as all who belong to Christ—both Jews and Gentiles—are part of God's unified people. Paul hints at this unity in passages like Ephesians 2:14-16, where he explains that through Christ's work on the cross, the "dividing wall" between Jew and Gentile has been broken down, and both are reconciled into one body.

- New Jerusalem and the Tribes of Israel: Revelation 21 describes the New Jerusalem, the eternal city where God dwells with His people. The city has twelve gates, and on these gates are written the names of the twelve tribes of Israel (Revelation 21:12). This imagery suggests that Israel's identity is honored in the eternal state, recognizing the role Israel played in God's redemptive plan. However, the city also has twelve foundations, and on these are written the names of the twelve apostles, signifying the inclusion of the church (Revelation 21:14).

- The New Heavens and New Earth: After the final rebellion and judgment, the creation of the new heavens and new earth marks the beginning of the eternal state (Revelation 21:1-5). In this new creation, Israel's unique role as God's chosen people in history transitions into its place as part of the universal body of believers who will dwell with God forever. The people of Israel, like all believers, will enjoy eternal life, free from sin, suffering, and death.

3. Israel's Role in the Eternal Worship of God

- Worship in the New Creation: In the new heavens and new earth, all of God's people—Jews and Gentiles—will worship Him together. The New Jerusalem is described as the central location where God dwells with His people. The entire city is filled with God's glory, and there is no need for a temple because "the Lord God Almighty and the Lamb are its temple" (Revelation 21:22). Israel, as part of the redeemed, will join in eternal worship and fellowship with God.

- Fulfillment of Prophetic Visions: Old Testament prophets like Isaiah and Ezekiel foresaw a time of ultimate peace and worship for Israel. In the eternal state, these visions are fulfilled as Israel, along with all the nations, participates in the worship of the one true God. The New Jerusalem is the place where people from all nations, including Israel, will bring their glory and honor into it (Revelation 21:24-26).

4. No National Distinction in the Eternal State

- Spiritual Unity: By the time of the eternal state, the distinct national identity of Israel, as we understand it from Scripture, merges into the larger identity of all the redeemed. The Bible emphasizes that in Christ, there is neither Jew nor Gentile (Galatians 3:28), but all are one in Him. The Millennial Kingdom may highlight Israel's distinct role, but after the millennium, the eternal state involves all of God's people living together without national distinctions.

- Inheritance for All Believers: Revelation describes the inheritance of all believers in the eternal state as being in the New Jerusalem. This city is open to all nations, and the Bible no longer emphasizes Israel as a separate nation but instead highlights the unity of all believers. Israel, having fulfilled its covenantal role, is now part of the greater redeemed community that enjoys eternal fellowship with God.

5. God's Faithfulness to Israel and the Church

- Covenantal Fulfillment: Even in the eternal state, the fact that the names of the twelve tribes of Israel are inscribed on the gates of the New Jerusalem signifies God's unbreakable faithfulness to Israel. Throughout history, Israel played a pivotal role in God's redemptive plan, leading to the coming of the Messiah, Jesus Christ.

- The Church and Israel as One Body: The New Testament teaches that the church has been grafted into the promises made to Israel (Romans 11). In the eternal state, both the church and Israel are part of one body, united in Christ, worshipping God forever. The church is not a replacement for Israel but rather shares in the fulfillment of God's redemptive plan alongside Israel.

Conclusion: Israel's Role After the Millennium

After the Millennium, Israel's role merges with the broader people of God in the eternal state. The promises made to Israel are fully realized in the Millennium, with Jesus reigning from Jerusalem and fulfilling the covenant promises. Once the eternal state begins after the Great White Throne Judgment and the creation of the new heavens and new earth, Israel joins the rest of redeemed humanity in eternal worship of God. In the New Jerusalem, the names of the twelve tribes of Israel are honored, but national distinctions fade as all believers—Jew and Gentile—share in the eternal inheritance promised by God. Israel's special role in redemptive history is forever acknowledged, but in the eternal state, all God's people are united in Christ, worshiping Him in perfect peace and righteousness.

TIMELINE OF KEY EVENTS

KEY EVENTS IN THE SEVENTY WEEKS PROPHECY

Timeline of Key Events

Key Events in the Seventy Weeks Prophecy:

1. Decree to Rebuild Jerusalem:

- 445 B.C.: Artaxerxes I issues a decree to Nehemiah to rebuild Jerusalem (Nehemiah 2:1-8).

2. First Seven Weeks (49 years):

- 445-396 B.C.: Period of rebuilding Jerusalem, including the completion of the walls and restoration efforts led by Nehemiah and Ezra.

3. Sixty-two Weeks (434 years):

- 396 B.C. - 27 A.D.: Period leading up to the ministry of Jesus Christ, including key events like the rise of the Roman Empire and the influence of Hellenistic culture.

- 4 B.C.: Birth of Jesus Christ.

- 27-30 A.D.: Ministry of Jesus Christ, including His baptism, teachings, miracles, crucifixion, and resurrection.

4. Final Week (7 years):

- 30 A.D. - Future: The cutting off of the Anointed One (crucifixion of Jesus) and subsequent events leading to the destruction of Jerusalem in A.D. 70 by the Romans.

- Future Fulfillment: Anticipated future events involving the Antichrist, tribulation, and the second coming of Christ.

Additional Historical Context

Babylonian Exile:

- 605-538 B.C.: Babylonian captivity of the Jewish people, during which Daniel lived and served in the Babylonian and Persian courts.

- 538 B.C.: Decree of Cyrus allowing the Jewish exiles to return to Jerusalem and rebuild the temple (Ezra 1:1-4).

Persian Period:

- 539-331 B.C.: Period of Persian dominance, marked by the rebuilding efforts in Jerusalem and the ministries of prophets like Haggai, Zechariah, and Malachi.

Hellenistic Period:

- 331-167 B.C.: Period of Greek influence following Alexander the Great's conquests, leading to the spread of Hellenistic culture and the translation of the Hebrew Scriptures into Greek (Septuagint).

Hasmonean Period:

- 167-63 B.C.: Jewish independence under the Hasmonean dynasty, initiated by the Maccabean Revolt and the rededication of the temple (Hanukkah).

Roman Period:

- 63 B.C. - 70 A.D.: Roman control over Judea, culminating in the destruction of Jerusalem and the temple in A.D. 70.

Intertestamental Period:

- 400 B.C. - 4 B.C.: The silent years between the Old and New Testaments, during which significant historical and cultural developments occurred, setting the stage for the New Testament era.

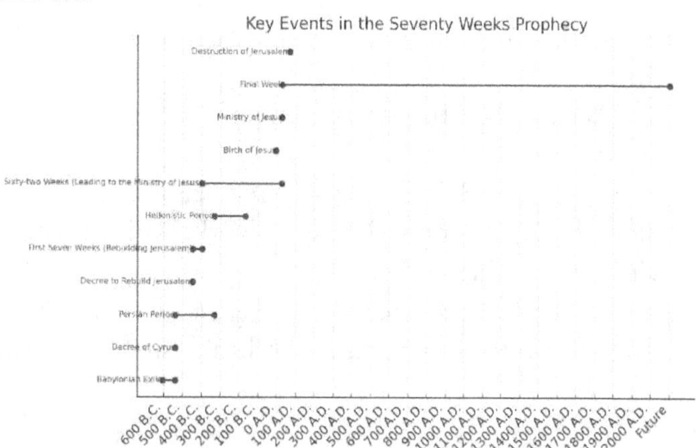

Charts and Diagrams
Chart: Timeline of Daniel's Seventy Weeks Prophecy

Period	Duration	Key Events
First Seven Weeks	49 years	Rebuilding of Jerusalem (445-396 B.C.)
Sixty-Two Weeks	434 years	Events leading up to Jesus' Ministry (396 B.C. – 27 A.D.)
Final Week	7 years	Crucifixion of Jesus, destruction of Jerusalem future events.

Diagram: Prophetic Timeline
1. First Seven Weeks (445-396 B.C.)
    - Decree to rebuild Jerusalem.
    - Completion of Jerusalem's walls and city restoration.
2. Sixty-two Weeks (396 B.C. - 27 A.D.)
    - Intertestamental developments.
    - Birth and ministry of Jesus Christ.
3. Final Week (30 A.D. - Future)
    - Crucifixion of Jesus.
    - Destruction of Jerusalem (70 A.D.).
    - Anticipated future tribulation and second coming of Christ.

Chart: Key Figures and Events

Figure/Event	Date	Significance
Decree by Artaxerxes I	445 B.C.	Start of the seventy weeks
Rebuilding of Jerusalem	445-396 B.C.	Fulfillment of the first seven weeks
Birth of Jesus Christ	4 B.C.	Fulfillment of messianic prophecies
Ministry of Jesus	27-30 A.D.	Crucifixion and resurrection
Destruction of Jerusalem	70 A.D.	Fulfillment of the prophecy regarding the destruction
Future Tribulation	Future	Anticipated events involving the Antichrist
Second Coming of Christ	Future	An ultimate fulfillment of God's redemptive plan

Diagram: The Seventy Weeks Prophecy Structure
1. First Seven Weeks:
    - Rebuilding efforts post-exile.
    - Leadership of Nehemiah and Ezra.
2. Sixty-Two Weeks:
    - Historical and cultural developments.
    - Messianic expectation and the life of Jesus.
3. Final Week:
    - Jesus' sacrificial death.
    - Destruction of Jerusalem.
    - Future eschatological events.

DANIEL'S 70-WEEK PROPHECY TIMELINE

70-WEEK PROPHECY TIMELINE

First Seven Weeks (49 years)

- Period: 445 B.C. - 396 B.C.

- Key Events: Decree to rebuild Jerusalem issued by Artaxerxes I; Rebuilding of Jerusalem's walls and city restoration.

- Meaning/Function: Restoration of Jerusalem's infrastructure and religious practices.

Sixty-Two Weeks (434 years)

- Period: 396 B.C. - 27 A.D.

- Key Events: Events leading up to the ministry of Jesus Christ; Influence of Hellenistic culture; Translation of Hebrew Scriptures into Greek (Septuagint); Rise of the Roman Empire.

- Meaning/Function: Preparation for the coming of the Messiah; Establishment of historical and cultural context for Jesus' ministry.

Final Week (7 years)

- Period: 27 A.D. - Future

- Key Events:

- First Half: Jesus' ministry and crucifixion ("cutting off of the Anointed One").

- Second Half: Destruction of Jerusalem and the temple by Romans in A.D. 70; Future events involving the Antichrist and tribulation; Anticipated second coming of Christ.

- Meaning/Function: Fulfillment of messianic prophecies through Jesus' atoning sacrifice; Future eschatological events leading to ultimate restoration and establishment of God's eternal kingdom.

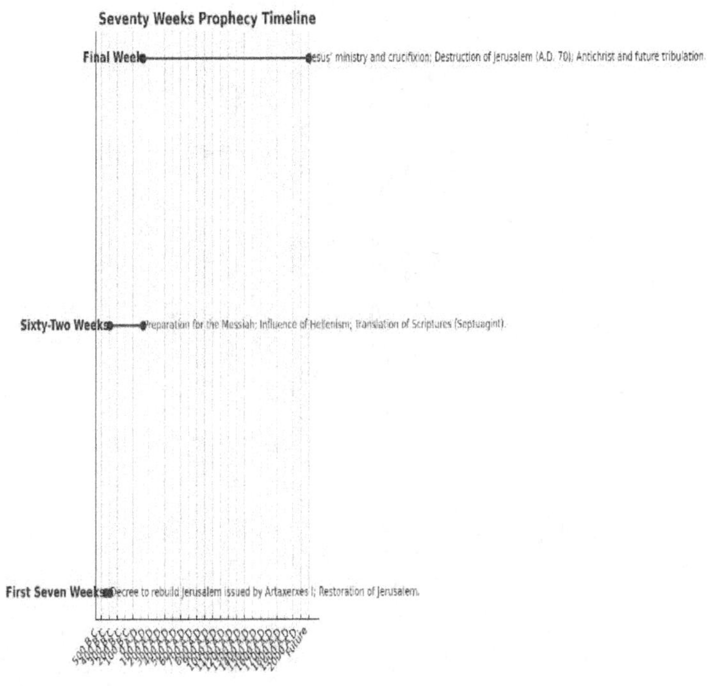

Seventy Weeks Prophecy Timeline
Final Week
Jesus' ministry and crucifixion; Destruction of Jerusalem (A.D. 70); Antichrist and future tribulation.
Sixty-Two Weeks
Preparation for the Messiah; Influence of Hellenism; Translation of Scriptures (Septuagint).
First Seven Weeks
Decree to rebuild Jerusalem issued by Artaxerxes I; Restoration of Jerusalem.

Daniel's 70 Weeks Prophecy

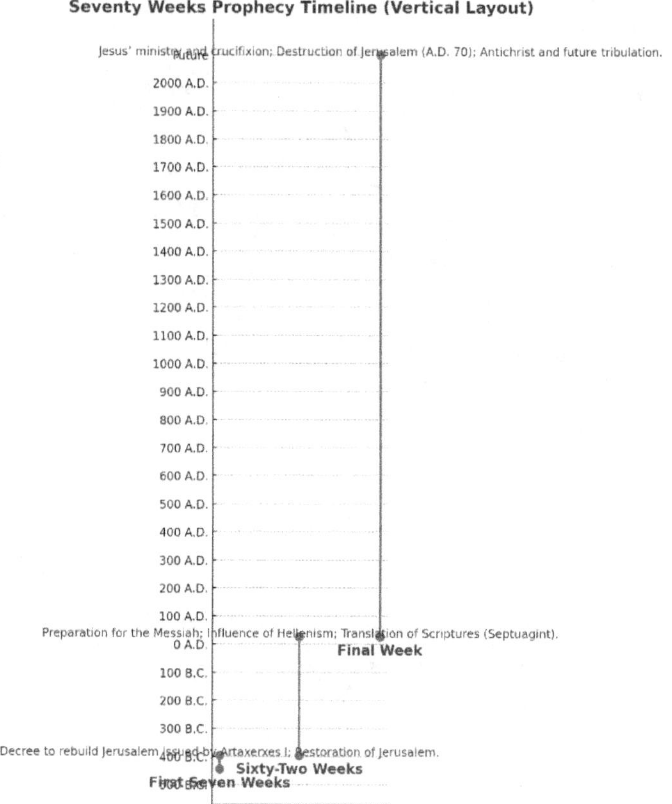

DANIEL CHAPTER NINE
COMMENTARY VERSE-BY-VERSE

THE 70-WEEK PROPHECY OF JEREMIAH

Chapter 9 of the Book of Daniel is a pivotal chapter that features Daniel's prayer and an angelic response. This chapter is often referred to as Daniel's prayer of confession and intercession. It takes place during the Babylonian exile when Daniel is reflecting on the prophecies of Jeremiah concerning the duration of Israel's captivity.

Daniel 9:1 (King James Version) states:

"In the first year of Darius the son of Ahasuerus, of the seed of the Medes, which was made king over the realm of the Chaldeans;"

This verse marks the beginning of Daniel's prayer and the context for the prophecy found in the later verses of Daniel 9. Let's break down the key elements:

1. "In the first year of Darius": This sets the time frame for the events described. Darius is identified as the son of Ahasuerus, commonly associated with the historical figure Darius the Mede, who succeeded Belshazzar and took over the Babylonian kingdom.

2. "which was made king over the realm of the Chaldeans": Darius took control of the Babylonian empire. This provides historical context for Daniel's prayer and the subsequent revelations he receives.

Daniel 9, as a whole, is a chapter known for Daniel's fervent prayer and the prophecy of the Seventy Weeks, which has been widely interpreted as a timeline leading to the Messiah. Daniel's prayer, which follows this verse, reflects repentance, confession of sin, and a plea for God's mercy and restoration.

The chapter as a whole contributes to the broader themes of Daniel, including God's sovereignty over nations, the fulfillment of prophecies, and the anticipation of the coming Messiah.

Daniel 9:2 (King James Version) states:

"In the first year of his reign I Daniel understood by books the number of the years, whereof the word of the Lord came to Jeremiah the prophet, that he would accomplish seventy years in the desolations of Jerusalem."

This verse provides insight into Daniel's understanding of the prophetic timeline and the context for his prayer. Let's break down the key components:

1. "In the first year of his reign": Referring to the first year of Darius's reign, as mentioned in the previous verse. This establishes the timing of Daniel's realization.

2. "I Daniel understood by books": Daniel, being a man of great wisdom and knowledge, turned to the Scriptures to seek understanding. The "books" likely refer to scrolls or writings available to him at that time.

3. "the number of the years, whereof the word of the Lord came to Jeremiah the prophet": Daniel refers to the prophecy of Jeremiah, particularly in Jeremiah 25:11-12 and 29:10. Jeremiah had prophesied that the desolation of Jerusalem would last seventy years, and Daniel, through studying these prophecies, gained insight into the timing of the exile.

4. "that he would accomplish seventy years in the desolations of Jerusalem": Daniel recognizes that the period of desolation is coming to an end after seventy years, as foretold by Jeremiah. This realization prompts Daniel's prayer for forgiveness, restoration, and the fulfillment of God's promises.

In essence, Daniel 9:2 underscores Daniel's deep understanding of prophecy, his reliance on the Scriptures, and his awareness of God's appointed times. This sets the stage for the heartfelt prayer and the subsequent revelation of the Seventy Weeks in Daniel 9.

Daniel 9:3 (King James Version) states:

"And I set my face unto the Lord God, to seek by prayer and supplications, with fasting, and sackcloth, and ashes."

This verse describes Daniel's response to understanding the prophecy of Jeremiah and the impending end of the seventy-year exile. Let's break down the key components:

1. "And I set my face unto the Lord God": Daniel turns his attention and focus completely toward God. This expression signifies a deep commitment and earnestness in seeking God's presence and guidance.

2. "to seek by prayer and supplications": Daniel's response is characterized by intense prayer and supplication. It reflects his humility and dependence on God. Supplication involves earnestly pleading and requesting, emphasizing the urgency and sincerity of Daniel's approach.

3. "with fasting, and sackcloth, and ashes": These are symbols of mourning, penitence, and humility. Fasting, wearing sackcloth (a coarse material associated with mourning), and ashes (symbolic of repentance) all convey the seriousness of Daniel's prayer. They are external expressions of an internal contrition and desire for God's mercy.

This verse paints a vivid picture of Daniel's spiritual posture—an earnest, humble, and repentant seeking of God through prayer, supplication, and acts of humility. Daniel's response sets an example for sincere and heartfelt seeking of God's guidance and mercy in times of realization, repentance, and anticipation of God's promised restoration.

Daniel 9:4 (King James Version) states:

"And I prayed unto the Lord my God, and made my confession, and said, O Lord, the great and dreadful God, keeping the covenant and mercy to them that love him, and to them that keep his commandments."

This verse marks the beginning of Daniel's prayer, expressing his humility, confession, and acknowledgment of God's attributes. Let's break down the key components:

1. "And I prayed unto the Lord my God": Daniel initiates his prayer, addressing God with a personal and intimate acknowledgment of the Lord as his own.

2. "and made my confession": Daniel humbly confesses his sins and the sins of his people. This confession is an integral part of his prayer, reflecting a repentant heart.

3. "O Lord, the great and dreadful God": Daniel acknowledges God's greatness and the awe-inspiring nature of His holiness. The term "dreadful" emphasizes the reverence and fear due to God.

4. "keeping the covenant and mercy to them that love him, and to them that keep his commandments": Daniel acknowledges God's faithfulness in keeping His covenant and extending mercy to those who love Him and follow His commandments. This emphasizes the relational aspect of God's covenant, where obedience is met with mercy.

In this verse, Daniel sets a tone of reverence, confession, and acknowledgment of God's attributes. His prayer reflects a deep understanding of God's character, faithfulness to His covenant, and the importance of genuine love and obedience. This lays the foundation for Daniel's petition for mercy, forgiveness, and the fulfillment of God's promises in the subsequent verses.

Daniel 9:5 (King James Version) states:

"We have sinned, and have committed iniquity, and have done wickedly, and have rebelled, even by departing from thy precepts and from thy judgments."

In this verse, Daniel continues his prayer by acknowledging the sins of himself and his people. Let's break down the key elements:

1. "We have sinned, and have committed iniquity, and have done wickedly, and have rebelled": Daniel uses a

comprehensive language to confess the various aspects of wrongdoing. "Sinned" refers to falling short of God's standard, "committed iniquity" implies gross injustice or immorality, "done wickedly" indicates a deliberate choice toward evil, and "rebelled" signifies a willful disobedience against God.

2. "even by departing from thy precepts and from thy judgments": Daniel identifies the root cause of their sins— they have strayed from God's commandments and judgments. This emphasizes the significance of obedience to God's revealed will.

This verse reflects Daniel's deep sense of repentance and responsibility. By using inclusive language like "we," Daniel identifies himself with the collective guilt of the people. The confession is not vague but specifies the nature of their transgressions, and it underscores the importance of adherence to God's precepts.

Daniel's prayer embodies a model of genuine repentance—acknowledging specific sins, recognizing their departure from God's commands, and expressing remorse for their disobedience. This confession sets the stage for Daniel's plea for God's mercy and the fulfillment of His promises in the subsequent verses.

Daniel 9:6 (King James Version) states:

"Neither have we hearkened unto thy servants the prophets, which spake in thy name to our kings, our princes, and our fathers, and to all the people of the land."

In this verse, Daniel continues the confession of sins by acknowledging their failure to listen to the prophets sent by God. Let's break down the key elements:

1. "Neither have we hearkened unto thy servants the prophets": Daniel admits the collective disobedience of the people in not paying attention to the messages delivered by God's chosen messengers—the prophets.

2. "which spake in thy name": These prophets were not delivering their own messages but were speaking on behalf of God. Ignoring their words was, therefore, a rejection of God's guidance.

3. "to our kings, our princes, and our fathers, and to all the people of the land": The prophets addressed various strata of society, from the leadership to the general population. The failure to heed their messages affected all levels of the community.

This verse emphasizes the continuity of God's attempts to guide and correct His people through the prophets. Despite this, the people persisted in disobedience. Daniel's acknowledgment of this failure reflects a deep awareness of the historical and ongoing rebellion against God's revealed will.

The confession not only points to past disobedience but also sets the stage for Daniel's plea for forgiveness and restoration in the subsequent verses. It underscores the importance of heeding God's word and the consequences of turning away from His guidance.

Daniel 9:7 (King James Version) states:

"O Lord, righteousness belongeth unto thee, but unto us confusion of faces, as at this day; to the men of Judah, and to the inhabitants of Jerusalem, and unto all Israel, that are near, and that are far off, through all the countries whither thou hast driven them, because of their trespass that they have trespassed against thee."

In this verse, Daniel contrasts the righteousness of God with the shame and confusion experienced by the people of Judah. Let's break down the key elements:

1. "O Lord, righteousness belongeth unto thee": Daniel acknowledges God's inherent righteousness. He affirms that righteousness is an essential attribute of God, highlighting His moral perfection and justice.

2. "but unto us confusion of faces, as at this day": In contrast to God's righteousness, Daniel recognizes the people's shame and disgrace. The phrase "confusion of faces" conveys a sense of embarrassment and dishonor.

3. "to the men of Judah, and to the inhabitants of Jerusalem, and unto all Israel": Daniel includes the entire community in this acknowledgment, emphasizing that the consequences of their disobedience extend to all the people.

4. "that are near, and that are far off, through all the countries whither thou hast driven them": The dispersion of the people throughout various lands is acknowledged, highlighting the consequences of their disobedience and the scattering of the nation.

5. "because of their trespass that they have trespassed against thee": The reason for their shame and dispersion is attributed to the people's trespasses against God. This points back to the acknowledgment of sin and disobedience.

In this verse, Daniel continues his confession, recognizing the righteousness of God and the shame that the people have brought upon themselves through their disobedience. This sets the stage for Daniel's plea for mercy and restoration in the subsequent part of his prayer.

Daniel 9:8 (King James Version) states:

"O Lord, to us belongeth confusion of face, to our kings, to our princes, and to our fathers, because we have sinned against thee."

In this verse, Daniel continues to express contrition and acknowledgment of the people's guilt before God. Let's break down the key elements:

1. "O Lord, to us belongeth confusion of face": Daniel reiterates the shame and disgrace of the people. "Confusion of face" implies a deep sense of embarrassment and humiliation.

2. "to our kings, to our princes, and to our fathers": Daniel extends the confession to all levels of leadership and authority within the community. The acknowledgment of guilt encompasses both the current generation and the preceding ones.

3. "because we have sinned against thee": The reason for their shame and humiliation is clearly stated—it is a result of their collective sin against God. This concise confession underscores the central theme of repentance and recognition of wrongdoing.

Daniel's prayer is marked by a profound sense of corporate responsibility. By including kings, princes, fathers, and the entire nation, he emphasizes the communal nature of their transgressions. The prayer reflects not only an acknowledgment of individual sins but also a recognition of the impact of those sins on the entire community.

This verse lays the groundwork for Daniel's plea for God's mercy and restoration, emphasizing the people's repentance and desire for reconciliation with God.

Daniel 9:9 (King James Version) states:

"To the Lord our God belong mercies and forgivenesses, though we have rebelled against him."

In this verse, Daniel acknowledges God's character as merciful and forgiving, even in the face of the people's rebellion. Let's break down the key elements:

1. "To the Lord our God belong mercies and forgivenesses": Daniel recognizes God's inherent nature of mercy and forgiveness. Despite the people's transgressions, God is characterized by His compassion and willingness to extend forgiveness.

2. "though we have rebelled against him": The acknowledgment of rebellion is a continuation of the confession of sins. Daniel emphasizes the contrast between God's mercies and forgiveness and the people's willful disobedience.

This verse highlights a crucial aspect of Daniel's theology—he understands that the foundation of hope for reconciliation lies in God's merciful and forgiving nature. Even when confronted with the consequences of their rebellion, Daniel looks to God's character as a source of hope and restoration.

The verse sets the stage for Daniel's appeal for mercy and restoration in the following verses, emphasizing that the basis of their plea is not their own merit but God's gracious nature. It reflects a deep understanding of the dynamics of repentance and the gracious response of a forgiving God.

Daniel 9:10 (King James Version) states:

"Neither have we obeyed the voice of the Lord our God, to walk in his laws, which he set before us by his servants the prophets."

In this verse, Daniel continues the confession of the people's disobedience by acknowledging their failure to heed God's voice and follow His laws. Let's break down the key elements:

1. "Neither have we obeyed the voice of the Lord our God": This phrase underscores the fundamental failure of the people—they have not listened to God's instructions. It reflects a disobedience that goes beyond mere actions to a rejection of divine guidance.

2. "to walk in his laws, which he set before us by his servants the prophets": Daniel specifies the disobedience— they have not followed God's laws as communicated through the prophets. This emphasizes the role of the prophets as messengers and the importance of God's revealed will in the form of laws.

This verse aligns with the broader theme of Daniel's prayer, which includes confession, repentance, and a plea for God's mercy. By admitting their failure to obey God's voice and laws, Daniel underscores the need for divine forgiveness and restoration.

The acknowledgment of disobedience also serves to highlight the contrast between God's righteous expectations and the people's shortcomings, reinforcing the need for mercy and grace. This verse sets the stage for Daniel's continued petition for God's favor and the fulfillment of His promises.

Daniel 9:11 (King James Version) states:

"Yea, all Israel have transgressed thy law, even by departing, that they might not obey thy voice; therefore the curse is poured upon us, and the oath that is written in the law of Moses the servant of God, because we have sinned against him."

In this verse, Daniel continues the confession, emphasizing the collective transgression of Israel and the resulting consequences. Let's break down the key elements:

1. "Yea, all Israel have transgressed thy law": Daniel broadens the scope of the confession, stating that the entire nation has violated God's law. This inclusive language underscores the corporate responsibility for disobedience.

2. "even by departing, that they might not obey thy voice": The nature of their transgression is highlighted—it involves a deliberate turning away from God and a refusal to heed His voice. The departure signifies a willful rebellion.

3. "therefore the curse is poured upon us": Daniel connects the disobedience to the consequences—they are experiencing the curse as a result of their collective sin. This aligns with the covenantal principle of blessings for obedience and curses for disobedience outlined in the Law of Moses.

4. "and the oath that is written in the law of Moses the servant of God": Daniel refers to the covenantal oath outlined in the Law of Moses, emphasizing the seriousness and binding nature of the covenant.

5. "because we have sinned against him": The acknowledgment of sin remains central to the confession.

Daniel reiterates the reason for their current predicament—they have sinned against God.

This verse deepens the sense of corporate repentance and underscores the cause-and-effect relationship between disobedience and the consequences stipulated in the covenant. The confession prepares the way for Daniel's plea for God's mercy and restoration in the subsequent part of the prayer.

Daniel 9:12 (King James Version) states:

"And he hath confirmed his words, which he spake against us, and against our judges that judged us, by bringing upon us a great evil: for under the whole heaven hath not been done as hath been done upon Jerusalem."

In this verse, Daniel continues to reflect on the consequences of Israel's disobedience and acknowledges the fulfillment of God's warnings. Let's break down the key elements:

1. "And he hath confirmed his words, which he spake against us": Daniel recognizes that God has been faithful in fulfilling His spoken words of warning and judgment against the people. This underscores the reliability and trustworthiness of God's promises, both in blessings and curses.

2. "and against the judges that judged us": The consequences of disobedience have not spared even those in positions of authority. Judges and leaders are included in the judgment, emphasizing the widespread impact of the people's rebellion.

3. "by bringing upon us a great evil": The acknowledgment of a "great evil" underscores the severity of the judgment that has befallen the nation. This aligns with the covenantal principle of consequential blessings and curses.

4. "for under the whole heaven hath not been done as hath been done upon Jerusalem": Daniel emphasizes the

uniqueness and severity of the judgment upon Jerusalem. This could refer to the extent of destruction and suffering experienced by the city, making it an unparalleled event.

This verse deepens the understanding of the consequences of Israel's disobedience, highlighting the fulfillment of God's warnings and the severity of the judgment. Daniel's reflection prepares the ground for his subsequent plea for God's mercy and restoration.

Daniel 9:13 (King James Version) states:

"As it is written in the law of Moses, all this evil comes upon us: yet made we not our prayer before the Lord our God, that we might turn from our iniquities, and understand thy truth."

In this verse, Daniel acknowledges the connection between the written law of Moses and the troubles that have befallen the people. Let's break down the key elements:

1. "As it is written in the law of Moses": Daniel refers to the covenantal stipulations and warnings outlined in the Law of Moses, particularly in passages like Leviticus 26 and Deuteronomy 28. These passages outline the blessings for obedience and the curses for disobedience.

2. "all this evil comes upon us": Daniel attributes the adversity and judgment the people are experiencing to the fulfillment of the written warnings in the Law of Moses. This underscores the serious nature of God's covenant and the consequences of disobedience.

3. "yet made we not our prayer before the Lord our God": Despite the troubles and the clear connection to disobedience, Daniel acknowledges that the people did not seek God through prayer. There was a failure to turn to God in repentance and seek His guidance.

4. "that we might turn from our iniquities, and understand thy truth": Daniel identifies the purpose of prayer—not only seeking deliverance from the consequences but also turning away from sin and gaining understanding of

God's truth. Repentance and seeking divine guidance are essential components of genuine prayer.

This verse reflects Daniel's deep understanding of the spiritual dynamics at play. It underscores the importance of acknowledging God's Word, recognizing the connection between actions and consequences, and the role of repentant prayer in seeking God's mercy and understanding. This sets the stage for Daniel's fervent intercession on behalf of the people.

Daniel 9:14 (King James Version) states:

"Therefore hath the Lord watched upon the evil, and brought it upon us: for the Lord our God is righteous in all his works which he doeth: for we obeyed not his voice."

In this verse, Daniel acknowledges the righteousness of God in allowing adversity to come upon the people due to their disobedience. Let's break down the key elements:

1. "Therefore hath the Lord watched upon the evil, and brought it upon us": Daniel attributes the Lord's watchfulness and active involvement in bringing the forewarned judgment upon the people. This emphasizes the divine agency in the unfolding events.

2. "for the Lord our God is righteous in all his works which he doeth": Daniel affirms God's righteousness in His actions. This implies that God's judgment is just and in accordance with His character. Even in allowing adversity, God's righteousness is maintained.

3. "for we obeyed not his voice": The reason for the adversity is reiterated—disobedience to God's voice. The acknowledgment of their failure to heed God's commands is crucial to understanding the justice of God's response.

This verse underscores the theological understanding that God's actions are rooted in righteousness and justice. The acknowledgment of their disobedience is coupled with an acceptance of God's righteous judgment. Daniel's recognition of these spiritual principles prepares the way for his heartfelt plea for God's mercy and restoration in the subsequent part of the prayer.

Daniel 9:15 (King James Version) states:

"And now, O Lord our God, that hast brought thy people forth out of the land of Egypt with a mighty hand, and hast gotten thee renown, as at this day; we have sinned, we have done wickedly."

In this verse, Daniel appeals to God's past acts of deliverance and confesses the sins of the people. Let's break down the key elements:

1. "And now, O Lord our God, that hast brought thy people forth out of the land of Egypt with a mighty hand": Daniel begins by recalling a foundational act of God's deliverance—the liberation of the Israelites from Egypt. This serves as a reminder of God's power and faithfulness in the past.

2. "and hast gotten thee renown, as at this day": The deliverance from Egypt brought renown or reputation to God. Daniel acknowledges that God's mighty acts were not only for the benefit of the people but also for the manifestation of His glory.

3. "we have sinned, we have done wickedly": Despite God's past acts of deliverance and the renown He gained through them, Daniel humbly confesses the ongoing sinfulness of the people. This confession includes both individual and collective wrongdoing.

This verse reflects a pattern in Daniel's prayer—recalling God's faithfulness in the past while honestly confessing the present sins of the people. It sets the stage for Daniel's plea for God's mercy and the fulfillment of His promises, drawing on the precedent of God's historical faithfulness.

Daniel 9:16 (King James Version) states:

"O Lord, according to all thy righteousness, I beseech thee, let thine anger and thy fury be turned away from thy city Jerusalem, thy holy mountain: because for our sins, and for the iniquities of our fathers, Jerusalem and thy people are become a reproach to all that are about us."

In this verse, Daniel pleads with God to turn away His anger from Jerusalem and seeks mercy for the city and its people. Let's break down the key elements:

1. "O Lord, according to all thy righteousness, I beseech thee": Daniel begins his plea by appealing to God's righteousness. He recognizes that any request for mercy is grounded in God's just and righteous nature.

2. "let thine anger and thy fury be turned away": Daniel acknowledges the divine anger and fury as a consequence of the people's disobedience. His plea is for a reversal of this judgment, asking God to turn away His wrath.

3. "from thy city Jerusalem, thy holy mountain": The focus of Daniel's plea is on Jerusalem, particularly the holy mountain, which likely refers to Mount Zion where the temple stood. Daniel emphasizes the sacred nature of the city and its significance in the worship of God.

4. "because for our sins, and for the iniquities of our fathers": Daniel reiterates the reason for the divine anger—the sins of the current generation and the sins of their forefathers. This confession includes a sense of collective responsibility.

5. "Jerusalem and thy people become a reproach to all that are about us": Daniel laments the current state of Jerusalem and its people, acknowledging that their disobedience has brought reproach and shame upon them in the eyes of surrounding nations.

This verse captures Daniel's heartfelt plea for God's mercy, grounded in an understanding of God's righteousness and a deep concern for the honor of Jerusalem and its people.

It sets the tone for the continued intercession and supplication in the prayer.

Daniel 9:17 (King James Version) states:

"Now, therefore, O our God, hear the prayer of thy servant, and his supplications, and cause thy face to shine upon thy sanctuary that is desolate for the Lord's sake."

In this verse, Daniel continues his prayer, making a specific request for God to hear and act in response to the desolation of the sanctuary. Let's break down the key elements:

1. "Now, therefore, O our God": Daniel transitions from confession and acknowledgment to making a specific plea. The phrase "now, therefore" signals a movement from acknowledging sin to seeking God's intervention.

2. "hear the prayer of thy servant, and his supplications": Daniel entreats God to listen to his prayer and supplications. This emphasizes the earnestness and intensity of Daniel's plea.

3. "cause thy face to shine upon thy sanctuary": The imagery of God's face shining upon the sanctuary is a metaphor for God's favor and presence. Daniel is asking for divine attention, favor, and restoration for the desolate sanctuary.

4. "that is desolate for the Lord's sake": Daniel underscores that the request is not for personal gain but for the Lord's sake. He seeks the restoration of the sanctuary for the honor and glory of God.

This verse reveals Daniel's deep concern for the state of the sanctuary and his desire for divine intervention. It reflects a genuine and humble plea for God's mercy, not just for the sake of the people but for the sake of God's reputation and the sanctity of the place of worship. This sets the stage for the continuation of Daniel's intercessory prayer.

Daniel 9:18 (King James Version) states:

"O my God, incline thine ear, and hear; open thine eyes, and behold our desolations, and the city which is called by thy name: for we do not present our supplications before thee for our righteousnesses, but for thy great mercies."

In this verse, Daniel continues his prayer with a plea for God to pay attention to the desolation of the city and the sanctuary. Let's break down the key elements:

1. "O my God, incline thine ear, and hear": Daniel expresses a heartfelt plea for God to attentively listen to his prayer. The language of "incline thine ear" conveys a sense of urgency and earnestness.

2. "open thine eyes, and behold our desolations, and the city which is called by thy name": Daniel asks God to see and take notice of the desolation, particularly the condition of the city that bears God's name. This emphasizes the connection between the desolation and God's reputation.

3. "for we do not present our supplications before thee for our righteousnesses": Daniel emphasizes that their prayer is not based on their own righteousness or merit. It reflects a humble acknowledgment of their unworthiness and a reliance on God's mercy.

4. "but for thy great mercies": The motive behind their supplication is the greatness of God's mercies. Daniel appeals to God's compassionate nature, recognizing that mercy is the basis for their hope and request.

This verse showcases Daniel's humble approach in prayer. He pleads for God's attention and mercy, acknowledging the dire state of the city and sanctuary and emphasizing their dependence on God's compassion rather than their own righteousness. This sets the tone for the subsequent portions of the prayer where Daniel continues to intercede for restoration and mercy.

Daniel 9:19 (King James Version) states:

"O Lord, hear; O Lord, forgive; O Lord, hearken and do; defer not, for thine own sake, O my God: for thy city and thy people are called by thy name."

In this verse, Daniel concludes his prayer with a series of earnest requests directed towards God. Let's break down the key elements:

1. "O Lord, hear": Daniel reiterates his plea for God to listen attentively to his prayer. This repetition underscores the urgency and importance of the request.

2. "O Lord, forgive": Daniel seeks God's forgiveness for the sins and transgressions of the people. This aligns with the earlier theme of repentance and acknowledgment of wrongdoing.

3. "O Lord, hearken and do": Daniel implores God not only to listen but also to take action in response to the supplications. This reflects a desire for divine intervention and mercy.

4. "defer not": Daniel urges God not to delay in responding. The phrase "defer not" emphasizes the immediacy of the need for God's intervention.

5. "for thine own sake, O my God": Daniel appeals to God's own sake, emphasizing that God's reputation and glory are at stake. This aligns with the earlier emphasis on God's name being associated with the city and the people.

6. "for thy city and thy people are called by thy name": The concluding phrase reiterates the connection between God's name and the city and people. Daniel emphasizes that God's honor is intertwined with the well-being of Jerusalem and its inhabitants.

This verse encapsulates Daniel's fervent plea for divine mercy, forgiveness, and intervention for the sake of God's name and the sanctity of the city and people called by His name. It serves as a powerful conclusion to Daniel's prayer of confession, repentance, and intercession.

Daniel 9:20 (King James Version) states:

"And whiles I was speaking, and praying, and confessing my sin and the sin of my people Israel, and presenting my supplication before the Lord my God for the holy mountain of my God;"

In this verse, Daniel provides additional context about the timing and content of his prayer. Let's break down the key elements:

1. "And whiles I was speaking, and praying, and confessing my sin and the sin of my people Israel": Daniel gives insight into the ongoing nature of his prayer. It wasn't a brief or casual petition but a continuous and earnest expression of confession, repentance, and intercession. The repeated confession emphasizes the depth of Daniel's contrition.

2. "and presenting my supplication before the Lord my God": In addition to confession, Daniel emphasizes the act of presenting his supplication or earnest requests before God. This reinforces the multifaceted nature of his prayer, encompassing confession, supplication, and intercession.

3. "for the holy mountain of my God": Daniel specifies the focus of his prayer—the holy mountain, likely referring to Mount Zion where the temple stood. This underscores the significance of the sanctuary in Daniel's supplications.

This verse provides a glimpse into the intensity and continuity of Daniel's prayer. It emphasizes the holistic approach he takes, combining confession, supplication, and intercession, all directed toward God for the sake of the holy mountain. The verse sets the stage for the remarkable response that Daniel receives from the angel Gabriel in the subsequent verses.

Daniel 9:21 (King James Version) states:

"Yea, whiles I was speaking in prayer, even the man Gabriel, whom I had seen in the vision at the beginning, being caused to fly swiftly, touched me about the time of the evening oblation."

This verse marks a significant moment in Daniel's prayer as the angel Gabriel appears in response. Let's break down the key elements:

1. "Yea, whiles I was speaking in prayer": The verse emphasizes the immediacy of Gabriel's response. While Daniel was still in the act of praying, the angel arrives.

2. "even the man Gabriel, whom I had seen in the vision at the beginning": Gabriel is identified as the angel Daniel had previously seen in a vision. This reference highlights the continuity of divine communication and the familiarity between Daniel and the angelic messenger.

3. "being caused to fly swiftly": The description of Gabriel being caused to fly swiftly underscores the supernatural nature of the angel's arrival. It conveys a sense of urgency and divine intervention.

4. "touched me about the time of the evening oblation": The timing of Gabriel's arrival is noted—it occurs around the time of the evening oblation or the evening sacrifice. This detail further emphasizes the connection between Daniel's prayer and the sacred rituals associated with the temple.

This verse sets the stage for the subsequent revelation that Gabriel delivers to Daniel. The immediate response to Daniel's prayer demonstrates the divine attentiveness and readiness to provide guidance and insight. The mention of Gabriel, a significant angelic figure in biblical narratives, adds weight to the unfolding events in the book of Daniel.

Daniel 9:21 (King James Version) states:

"Yea, while I was speaking in prayer, even the man Gabriel, whom I had seen in the vision at the beginning, being caused to fly swiftly, touched me about the time of the evening oblation."

This verse marks a crucial moment in Daniel's prayer, as the angel Gabriel appears in response. Let's delve into the key elements:

1. "Yea, while I was speaking in prayer": The immediacy of Gabriel's appearance during Daniel's prayer underscores the responsiveness of divine intervention. It signifies a direct connection between Daniel's earnest supplication and the angelic response.

2. "even the man Gabriel, whom I had seen in the vision at the beginning": Gabriel is identified as the same angel Daniel encountered in an earlier vision. This continuity emphasizes the significance of Gabriel as a messenger with a specific role in conveying divine revelations.

3. "being caused to fly swiftly": The description of Gabriel being caused to fly swiftly highlights the supernatural nature of the angel's arrival. The swiftness of Gabriel's appearance suggests urgency and divine purpose.

4. "touched me about the time of the evening oblation": The timing of Gabriel's touch, occurring around the time of the evening oblation or sacrifice, adds a ceremonial dimension to the encounter. This temporal reference aligns with the sacred rhythms of Jewish worship.

The verse sets the stage for the subsequent revelation that Gabriel imparts to Daniel. The specific details surrounding Gabriel's arrival highlight the immediate response to Daniel's prayer and foreshadow the importance of the message that follows. The angelic visitation becomes a pivotal moment in the unfolding narrative of Daniel's prophetic visions.

Daniel 9:22 (King James Version) states:

"And he informed me, and talked with me, and said, O Daniel, I am now come forth to give thee skill and understanding."

In this verse, Gabriel begins to convey a message to Daniel, indicating the purpose of his visit. Let's break down the key elements:

1. "And he informed me, and talked with me": Gabriel takes on the role of an informant, sharing knowledge and engaging in dialogue with Daniel. This reflects the angel's function as a messenger delivering a specific message.

2. "and said, O Daniel": The personal address to Daniel adds a touch of intimacy and emphasizes the individual nature of the revelation. Gabriel's use of Daniel's name underscores a personal connection between the two.

3. "I am now come forth to give thee skill and understanding": Gabriel explicitly states the purpose of his visit—to provide Daniel with skill and understanding. This signifies a divine impartation of wisdom and insight beyond Daniel's human capacity.

The verse highlights the dynamic interaction between the angelic messenger and Daniel, setting the stage for the revelation that follows. Gabriel's mission is to equip Daniel with knowledge and understanding, emphasizing the divine intention to share insights into the unfolding prophetic events.

Daniel 9:23 (King James Version) states:

"At the beginning of thy supplications the commandment came forth, and I have come to show thee; for thou art greatly beloved: therefore understand the matter, and consider the vision."

In this verse, Gabriel provides additional context regarding the timing of his response to Daniel's prayer and the reason for his visit. Let's break down the key elements:

1. "At the beginning of thy supplications the commandment came forth": Gabriel reveals that the divine commandment to respond to Daniel's supplications was issued at the very start of Daniel's prayer. This underscores

the immediacy and priority of God's response to Daniel's heartfelt prayer.

2. "and I am come to show thee": Gabriel emphasizes his purpose—to reveal and explain certain matters to Daniel. This aligns with the earlier statement that he came to give Daniel skill and understanding.

3. "for thou art greatly beloved": Gabriel provides a profound insight into Daniel's relationship with God. Daniel is described as "greatly beloved," highlighting the divine favor and affection directed towards him.

4. "therefore understand the matter, and consider the vision": Gabriel urges Daniel to comprehend the information he is about to impart. The encouragement to "consider the vision" emphasizes the importance of reflection and understanding regarding the prophetic insights that will be revealed.

This verse unveils the divine response to Daniel's prayer, emphasizing God's immediate attention, Daniel's favored status, and the forthcoming revelation of important visions. It sets the stage for the detailed prophetic message that Gabriel delivers to Daniel in the subsequent verses.

Daniel 9:24 (King James Version) states:

"Seventy weeks are determined upon thy people and upon thy holy city, to finish the transgression, and to make an end of sins, and to make reconciliation for iniquity, and to bring in everlasting righteousness, and to seal up the vision and prophecy, and to anoint the most Holy."

This verse contains a highly significant and complex prophecy commonly known as the "Seventy Weeks Prophecy." Let's break down the key elements:

1. "Seventy weeks are determined upon thy people and upon thy holy city": The timeframe is specified as seventy weeks. In prophetic language, a day often represents a year, leading to an interpretation of 70 weeks or 490 years.

2. "to finish the transgression, and to make an end of sins": The prophecy foretells the completion or fulfillment of transgression and sins. This points to a future state where sin will be decisively dealt with.

3. "and to make reconciliation for iniquity": The prophecy anticipates the act of reconciliation for iniquity. This foreshadows a redemptive event that addresses the consequences of iniquity.

4. "and to bring in everlasting righteousness": A future era of everlasting righteousness is foretold. This suggests a time when God's righteousness will prevail permanently.

5. "and to seal up the vision and prophecy": The completion or sealing of the vision and prophecy is mentioned. This indicates that the revealed divine plan will be fully accomplished.

6. "and to anoint the most Holy": The prophecy concludes with the anointing of the most Holy. This could refer to the consecration or setting apart of a sacred place or person.

The Seventy Weeks Prophecy is intricate and has been subject to various interpretations. It is commonly understood to point to the coming of the Messiah, specifically Jesus Christ, and the redemptive work accomplished through His life, death, and resurrection. The fulfillment of these prophetic elements is viewed as spanning from the decree to rebuild Jerusalem to the time of Christ.

This verse marks a pivotal moment in the Book of Daniel, revealing God's plan for the redemption and restoration of His people. It serves as a foundation for understanding the broader prophetic context of the book.

Daniel 9:25 (King James Version) states:

"Know therefore and understand, that from the going forth of the commandment to restore and to build Jerusalem unto the Messiah the Prince shall be seven weeks, and threescore and two weeks: the street shall be built again, and the wall, even in troublous times."

This verse provides more details regarding the timing of the Seventy Weeks Prophecy and introduces the concept of weeks as units of time. Let's break down the key elements:

1. "Know therefore and understand": Gabriel encourages Daniel to comprehend the forthcoming revelation, emphasizing its significance and the need for understanding.

2. "from the going forth of the commandment to restore and to build Jerusalem": The starting point of the prophecy is identified—a decree to restore and rebuild Jerusalem. Historically, this decree is often associated with the decree of King Artaxerxes I to Nehemiah.

3. "unto the Messiah the Prince shall be seven weeks, and threescore and two weeks": The period is divided into two segments—seven weeks (49 years) and sixty-two weeks (434 years), totaling sixty-nine weeks (483 years). This period is understood by many scholars as leading to the arrival of the Messiah.

4. "the street shall be built again, and the wall, even in troublous times": During this period, Jerusalem will undergo a process of restoration, including the rebuilding of streets and walls, despite facing challenges and troubles.

The interpretation of this verse often aligns with the coming of Jesus Christ as the Messiah. The period of sixty-nine weeks is calculated from the decree to rebuild Jerusalem to the time of Jesus' ministry. The specific mention of the Messiah the Prince underscores the significance of this prophecy in pointing to the arrival of the promised Redeemer.

This verse lays out a detailed timeline within the Seventy Weeks Prophecy, connecting historical events to the coming of the Messiah. It serves as a key component in understanding the prophetic framework outlined in Daniel 9.

Daniel 9:26 (King James Version) states:

"And after threescore and two weeks shall Messiah be cut off, but not for himself: and the people of the prince that shall come shall destroy the city and the sanctuary, and the end thereof shall be with a flood, and unto the end of the war desolations are determined."

This verse continues the prophecy, focusing on events after the sixty-two weeks. Let's break down the key elements:

1. "And after threescore and two weeks shall Messiah be cut off": After the completion of the sixty-two weeks (which, together with the earlier seven weeks, makes a total of sixty-nine weeks), the prophecy foretells the cutting off or death of the Messiah. This is a significant and poignant event.

2. "but not for himself": The Messiah's death is not for His own sake but carries a redemptive purpose. This foreshadows the sacrificial nature of Jesus' death for the atonement of sins.

3. "and the people of the prince that shall come shall destroy the city and the sanctuary": Following the Messiah's death, a future event is prophesied—the destruction of Jerusalem and the sanctuary. Historical fulfillment is often associated with the Roman destruction of Jerusalem in AD 70.

4. "and the end thereof shall be with a flood": The destruction is described vividly, with the metaphor of a flood symbolizing a swift and overwhelming force.

5. "and unto the end of the war desolations are determined": The consequences of this war and destruction are far-reaching, leading to a state of desolation that persists.

This verse is intricately connected to the historical events surrounding the life, death, and resurrection of Jesus Christ. The destruction of Jerusalem by the Romans is seen as a fulfillment of this prophecy, emphasizing the consequences of rejecting the Messiah.

Overall, Daniel 9:26 provides a prophetic glimpse into the redemptive work of the Messiah, coupled with the subsequent judgment and desolation associated with the destruction of Jerusalem. It adds layers of depth to the overarching Seventy-Week Prophecy.

Daniel 9:27 (King James Version) states:

Daniel 9:27 is a significant and often debated verse within the Seventy Weeks Prophecy, which reads:

"And he shall confirm the covenant with many for one week: and in the midst of the week he shall cause the sacrifice and the oblation to cease, and for the overspreading of abominations he shall make it desolate, even until the consummation, and that determined shall be poured upon the desolate." (KJV)

Traditional Interpretation

In traditional dispensational interpretations, this verse is often understood as referring to the Antichrist, who will supposedly make a covenant with Israel during a future seven-year tribulation period. Midway through, the Antichrist is believed to break the covenant, causing sacrifices to cease and leading to great desolation. However, an alternate and compelling view proposes that the "he" in Daniel 9:27 is not the Antichrist, but rather Jesus Christ, the Messiah.

Jesus as the Covenant Confirming One

1. The Subject of the Prophecy: The Messiah

The context of Daniel 9:24-26 centers on the Messiah. Verse 26 explicitly mentions that the Messiah would be "cut off" (interpreted as the crucifixion of Jesus). It is logical to assume that verse 27 continues with the same subject, namely the Messiah. This reading sees Jesus as the one who "confirms the covenant with many."

- The term "confirm" implies the strengthening or affirmation of an existing covenant, not the creation of a new one. This is consistent with the mission of Jesus, who came to fulfill the promises made to the Jewish people through the Abrahamic and Mosaic covenants (see Matthew 5:17). Through His ministry and the new covenant in His blood (Luke 22:20), He confirmed God's promises to His people.

2. The Covenant with Many

The "many" referenced in Daniel 9:27 could be understood as the people of Israel or all believers in Christ. Jesus' ministry primarily focused on the Jews (Matthew 15:24), but the Gospel also extended to the Gentiles, fulfilling the promise made to Abraham that all nations would be blessed through him (Genesis 12:3). This aligns with Jesus confirming a covenant with "many."

3. Causing Sacrifices and Oblations to Cease

This aspect of the prophecy is seen as fulfilled by Jesus through His atoning death on the cross. According to the New Testament, Jesus' sacrifice once and for all put an end to the need for the Old Testament system of sacrifices (Hebrews 10:12-14). The "ceasing" of sacrifices is not due to the destruction by the Antichrist but because Jesus' ultimate sacrifice rendered the temple sacrifices obsolete.

4. In the Midst of the Week

Daniel 9:27 indicates that "in the midst of the week" (the final seven-year period), the one confirming the covenant would cause the sacrifices to cease. Jesus' ministry lasted approximately three and a half years, which aligns with the "midst of the week." His crucifixion occurred at this midpoint, fulfilling the prophecy by ending the Old Covenant sacrificial system.

5. Desolation and Abominations

After Jesus' death, Jerusalem and the temple were destroyed in A.D. 70, as prophesied. This destruction can be seen as the fulfillment of the "abominations that cause desolation," referred to in Daniel 9:27 and elaborated on by Jesus in Matthew 24:15, where He references the destruction of the temple. The desolation was the result of the Jewish rejection of the Messiah, leading to God's judgment on the city.

Theological Implications of This View

- Messiah-Centric Fulfillment: This interpretation maintains the focus on Jesus as the fulfillment of the prophecy, emphasizing His redemptive work rather than shifting focus to an Antichrist figure in the future. It stresses the finality of Christ's atoning work and the resulting obsolescence of the temple sacrifices.

- Historical Context: By understanding the destruction of Jerusalem in A.D. 70 as part of this prophecy, it provides a direct fulfillment within the historical timeframe of the early church. It negates the need to project these events into a distant future, focusing instead on the events surrounding Christ's first coming.

Viewing Jesus as the "one who will confirm the covenant" in Daniel 9:27 aligns with the overall messianic focus of the prophecy and maintains a Christ-centered interpretation. Jesus' ministry, death, and the establishment of the New Covenant bring an end to the sacrificial system, fulfilling the prophetic timeline of Daniel. This interpretation underscores the finality of Christ's work and His role in fulfilling Old Testament prophecy, rather than introducing the Antichrist into this key passage.

DANIEL CHAPTER NINE

SUMMARY

Expository - Book of Daniel Chapter 9:

Verses 1-2: "In the first year of Darius son of Xerxes (a Mede by descent), who was made ruler over the Babylonian kingdom—in the first year of his reign, I, Daniel, understood from the Scriptures, according to the word of the Lord given to Jeremiah the prophet, that the desolation of Jerusalem would last seventy years."

Daniel begins by mentioning the context of the chapter: the first year of Darius's reign over Babylon. He refers to the prophecies of Jeremiah that indicated a seventy-year period of desolation for Jerusalem due to the disobedience of the Israelites. Daniel recognizes this time as approaching its fulfillment.

Verses 3-19: Daniel's Prayer of Confession and Intercession Daniel offers a heartfelt prayer, confessing the sins of his people and acknowledging their disobedience to God's commands. He pleads for God's mercy and forgiveness, acknowledging God's righteousness and his people's unfaithfulness. Daniel's prayer is a model of humility, confession, and intercession on behalf of the nation.

Verses 20-23: The Angel Gabriel's Response As Daniel is still praying, the angel Gabriel is sent to him. Gabriel provides understanding and insight into the vision Daniel received in the previous chapter. He explains the significance of the seventy-year period mentioned by Jeremiah and reveals that God's plan for Jerusalem's restoration and the fulfillment of His promises is about to unfold.

Verses 24-27: The Prophecy of the Seventy Weeks Gabriel reveals a remarkable prophecy concerning seventy "weeks" (a symbolic time period) that is divided into three segments: seven weeks, sixty-two weeks, and one final week. These weeks are often interpreted as representing a total of

490 years. The prophecy outlines the events leading up to the coming of the Messiah, His death, and the subsequent events related to Jerusalem and the people of Israel.

Commentary: Chapter 9 of Daniel is a profound blend of personal prayer, national confession, divine response, and prophetic revelation. It showcases Daniel's deep spiritual understanding and his concern for the welfare of his people. The chapter also provides a fascinating insight into God's intricate plan for redemption, including the eventual arrival of the Messiah.

Daniel's prayer demonstrates the principle of humility and confession before God, even when interceding for a nation. His understanding of the Scriptures, particularly the prophecies of Jeremiah, informs his prayer and leads to God's revelation through the angel Gabriel.

The prophecy of the seventy weeks is one of the most significant prophetic passages in the Bible, pointing to the coming of Christ and the events surrounding His ministry, crucifixion, and the future restoration of Jerusalem. The chapter serves as a bridge connecting historical events with messianic prophecies and anticipations.

Daniel Chapter 9 is a pivotal chapter that blends prayer, confession, divine response, and prophetic revelation. It underscores the themes of humility, confession, God's sovereign plan, and the redemptive work of the Messiah. This chapter is a testament to Daniel's faithfulness and the depth of his relationship with God.

DANIEL CHAPTER NINE

PROPHECY

Daniel 9 encompasses two significant prophecies: the first spanning 70 years and the second covering 70 weeks. This article will concentrate on the first prophecy.

Daniel's Attention to Jeremiah's 70-Year Prophecy

Regarding the initial prophecy, Daniel recorded, "In the first year of Darius the son of Ahasuerus ... I, Daniel, understood by the books the number of the years specified by the word of the LORD through Jeremiah the prophet, that He would accomplish seventy years in the desolations of Jerusalem" (Daniel 9:1-2).

Daniel's mention of "the books" pertains to the prophecies conveyed by God through Jeremiah. The specific prophecy Daniel referred to was one delivered in Jerusalem just before the Babylonian invasion and subsequently relayed through a letter from Jerusalem to the Babylonian captives (Jeremiah 25:1-11; 29:1-10).

This prophecy predicted that the "land shall be a desolation," and the Jewish people would "serve the king of Babylon seventy years" (Jeremiah 25:11; compare 2 Chronicles 36:17-21). Following the completion of these 70 years in Babylon, God assured them that He would "cause them to return to this place [Jerusalem]" (Jeremiah 29:10).

This prophecy contained two distinct elements: the "desolation" of the land and the servitude to the king of Babylon (Jeremiah 25:11). It appears that each aspect was fulfilled over slightly different but overlapping 70-year periods.

The 70 years of desolation of the land can be calculated as the period between the destruction of the temple by the Babylonians, which indeed resulted in a desolate state for Jerusalem and the subsequent reconstruction of the temple.

The captivity of the Jewish people, commencing before the temple's destruction with the initial deportation of Jews to Babylon and concluding with a decree issued by Cyrus permitting the Jews to return to Jerusalem, also spanned 70 years.

The timeline of the Babylonian exile unfolds as follows:

The initial deportation of Jews to Babylon, which included figures like Daniel and his companions Shadrach, Meshach, and Abed-Nego, marked the commencement of the 70-year captivity. Bible scholars generally place this event between 607 and 605 B.C.

The return of the Jews to Jerusalem took place approximately between 539 and 536 B.C., signifying the end of the captivity.

Regarding the period spanning the destruction and subsequent reconstruction of the temple, commonly referenced dates range from 586 or 585 to 516 or 515 B.C. While pinpointing exact years may prove challenging, these frequently cited timeframes align with the prophesied 70 years.

The Expositor's Bible Commentary underscores the significance of these stages of the Captivity in calculating the seventy years of exile foretold in Jeremiah 29:10. The interval between the first deportation in 605 B.C., involving Daniel himself, and the return of the exiles under Zerubbabel to establish an altar in Jerusalem in 536 B.C. indeed amounted to seventy years. Similarly, the period spanning the destruction of the first temple by Nebuzaradan in 586 and the completion of the second temple by Zerubbabel in 516 encompassed about seventy years (comments on Daniel 1:1-2).

The 70 years of captivity endured by the people of Judah were a consequence of their disobedience to God's commandments and laws. As Jeremiah conveyed to them, despite God's consistent efforts through His prophets to warn and guide them, they had chosen not to listen or pay heed (Jeremiah 25:3-4).

The sins of Judah encompassed wicked actions and the practice of idolatry (Jeremiah 25:5-7). The significance of the 70-year duration may lie in its alignment with the number of violations committed by the people of Judah against God's directive for the land to observe a Sabbath rest every seventh year (Leviticus 25:1-7, 20-22; 26:33-35; 2 Chronicles 36:20-21). According to the Jamieson, Fausset, and Brown Commentary, these 70 years correspond to the exact count of Sabbaths within the 490-year period stretching from Saul to the Babylonian captivity.

The commentary further suggests that the 70 years likely commenced from the fourth year of Jehoiakim, when Jerusalem was initially captured, resulting in the deportation of many captives and the seizure of temple treasures. The 70-year span came to a close with the first year of Cyrus, who, upon conquering Babylon, issued an edict for the restoration of the Jewish people (Ezra 1:1) (comments on Jeremiah 25:11).

Daniel lives through in the 70-year punishment

Daniel 1:21 explains that "Daniel continued until the first year of Cyrus"—which was the year Cyrus made a proclamation allowing the Jews to return to Jerusalem and rebuild the temple. The year of this proclamation marked the end of the 70-year captivity of the Jews predicted by God through Jeremiah.

This passage tells us that Daniel lived in Babylon throughout the entire 70 years of the Jewish captivity. He lived to see the fall of the Babylonian Empire and the sudden rise of the Medo-Persian Empire with its first ruler, Cyrus.

One of King Cyrus's initial actions was to issue a decree permitting the Jews to depart from Babylon. This momentous occasion is recorded in the book of Ezra, which describes the joyful event for the Jewish people in the following manner: "In the first year of Cyrus king of Persia, that the word of the LORD by the mouth of Jeremiah might be fulfilled, the LORD stirred up the spirit of Cyrus king of Persia, so that he made a proclamation throughout all his kingdom, and also put it in writing, saying,

"'Thus says Cyrus king of Persia: All the kingdoms of the earth the LORD God of heaven has given me. And He has commanded me to build Him a house at Jerusalem which is in Judah. Who is among you of all His people? May his God be with him, and let him go up to Jerusalem which is in Judah, and build the house of the LORD God of Israel (He is God), which is in Jerusalem'" (Ezra 1:1-3).

It is interesting to note that over 150 years in advance, God foretold the birth of Cyrus and what this king would do. Through the prophet Isaiah, God said, "Thus says the LORD to His anointed, to Cyrus, whose right hand I have held—to subdue nations before him and loose the armor of kings, to open before him the double doors, so that the gates will not be shut: 'I will go before you and make the crooked places straight; I will break in pieces the gates of bronze and cut the bars of iron.

"'I will give you the treasures of darkness and hidden riches of secret places, that you may know that I, the LORD, who call you by your name, am the God of Israel. For Jacob My servant's sake, and Israel My elect, I have even called you by your name; I have named you, though you have not known Me" (Isaiah 45:1-4).

In advance of the punishment, He would bring on Jacob's descendants—the people of Judah—God planned for the man who would eventually come to power and release the Jews from captivity.

Daniel's realization of how God was fulfilling Jeremiah's 70-year prophecy had a profound impact on him. Daniel 9:3-19 records Daniel's heartfelt prayer, where he confesses the national sins of Judah and pleads for God's forgiveness and assistance.

One of the primary lessons we can draw from this prophecy against Judah is God's requirement of obedience to His laws. This expectation applied especially to the descendants of Abraham, who later became known as Israelites and, subsequently, the kingdoms of Israel and Judah after the nation split into two. The blessings for obedience and the consequences of disobedience outlined in Leviticus 26 and Deuteronomy 28 continued to apply to these people.

Regrettably, the descendants of the ancient Israelites have persistently disobeyed God's laws. Similar to what transpired during the 70-year prophecy for the kingdom of Judah, these people will face divine punishment once again due to their refusal to follow God's timeless commandments. To gain more insight into the identity of these people and what has been prophesied for them, please refer to the articles in the sections "12 Tribes of Israel" and "Where Is America in Prophecy?"

Another crucial lesson for us stems from Daniel's response to Jeremiah's 70-year prophecy. Just as Daniel, through the study of God's Word, discerned where he stood in the biblical prophecy's timeline, Jesus Christ urges us to recognize "the signs of the times" in our era (Matthew 16:1-3).

Do you have an understanding of where we are in prophecy? Are you aware of the events that must unfold before the return of Jesus Christ to Earth? Most importantly, do you know what God expects from you?

Finally, this account highlights one more aspect that deserves our attention: the wonderful future that God had prepared for His people after their 70-year captivity in Babylon came to an end.

In one of the most frequently quoted passages in the Bible, God assured the people of Judah with these words: "For I know the thoughts that I think toward you, says the LORD, thoughts of peace and not of evil, to give you a future and a hope" (Jeremiah 29:11).

These words were delivered to the people of Judah during their time of captivity and were meant to provide them with hope and encouragement. However, it's essential to carefully consider the future that God envisioned for these people.

"Then you will call upon Me and go and pray to Me, and I will listen to you. And you will seek Me and find Me when you search for Me with all your heart. I will be found by you, says the LORD, and I will bring you back from your captivity; I will gather you from all the nations and from all the places where I have driven you, says the LORD, and I will bring you to the place from which I caused you to be carried away captive" (verses 12-14).

God's anticipation was that these people would earnestly seek Him, and in return, He would bless them. God has the same desire for all people, including each of us today. He longs for a similar future with each of us, but it requires our response to God by loving Him and fulfilling His purpose for our lives.

BIBLIOGRAPHY

SCHOLARLY SOURCES AND COMMENTARIES

Scholarly Sources and Commentaries

1. Baldwin, Joyce G.. Daniel: An Introduction and Commentary. InterVarsity Press, 1978.

- A comprehensive commentary on the Book of Daniel, providing historical context, theological insights, and detailed analysis of the text.

2. Goldingay, John E.. Daniel. Word Biblical Commentary, Vol. 30. Thomas Nelson, 1989.

- An in-depth scholarly commentary offering linguistic, historical, and theological perspectives on Daniel's prophecies.

3. Longman III, Tremper. Daniel: The NIV Application Commentary. Zondervan, 1999.

- A balanced commentary that bridges the original context of Daniel with contemporary application for modern readers.

4. Lucas, Ernest C.. Daniel. Apollos Old Testament Commentary. InterVarsity Press, 2002.

- A detailed examination of the Book of Daniel, focusing on its historical background and prophetic messages.

5. Miller, Stephen R.. Daniel. The New American Commentary, Vol. 18. B&H Publishing Group, 1994.

- A conservative evangelical commentary providing clear exposition and practical insights on the Book of Daniel.

6. Steinmann, Andrew E.. Daniel. Concordia Commentary. Concordia Publishing House, 2008.

- A theological and exegetical commentary that emphasizes the Christological aspects of Daniel's prophecies.

7. Towner, W. Sibley. Daniel: Interpretation: A Bible Commentary for Teaching and Preaching. Westminster John Knox Press, 1984.

- A commentary designed for pastors and teachers, offering accessible explanations and homiletical insights.

8. Young, Edward J.. The Prophecy of Daniel: A Commentary. Eerdmans, 1949.

- A classic commentary that explores the prophetic and apocalyptic dimensions of Daniel's visions.

Further Reading

1. Beale, G.K., and Carson, D.A. (Eds.). Commentary on the New Testament Use of the Old Testament. Baker Academic, 2007.

- A resource that examines how New Testament writers used and interpreted Old Testament prophecies, including those in Daniel.

2. Collins, John J.. Daniel: With an Introduction to Apocalyptic Literature. The Forms of the Old Testament Literature Series, Vol. 20. Eerdmans, 1984.

- An introduction to the apocalyptic genre and its manifestation in the Book of Daniel.

3. Freedman, David Noel, et al. (Eds.). The Anchor Yale Bible Dictionary. 6 vols. Yale University Press, 1992.

- A comprehensive dictionary providing detailed entries on the historical, cultural, and theological aspects of biblical texts, including Daniel.

4. Pfeiffer, Charles F.. Old Testament History. Baker Book House, 1973.

- A historical overview of the Old Testament, offering context for understanding the background of Daniel's prophecies.

5. Wenham, Gordon J.. Exploring the Old Testament: A Guide to the Pentateuch. IVP Academic, 2003.

- An introductory guide to the first five books of the Old Testament, providing foundational knowledge for understanding biblical prophecy.

6. Wright, N.T.. The Resurrection of the Son of God. Fortress Press, 2003.

- A comprehensive study of the resurrection, exploring its implications for understanding messianic prophecies and the fulfillment of God's plan.

7. Yamauchi, Edwin M.. Persia and the Bible. Baker Academic, 1990.

- An exploration of the Persian Empire's influence on the biblical world, particularly relevant for understanding the context of Daniel's ministry and prophecies.

8. Zimmerli, Walther. The Fiery Throne: The Prophets and Old Testament Theology. Fortress Press, 2003.

- A study of Old Testament prophecy and its theological significance, offering insights into the role of prophets like Daniel.

www.ingramcontent.com/pod-product-compliance
Lightning Source LLC
Chambersburg PA
CBHW071950150726
47999CB00001B/378